P9-CFI-231

Integrative Group Treatment for Bulimia Nervosa

Integrative Group Treatment for Bulimia Nervosa

Helen Riess, M.D.
and Mary Dockray-Miller

Columbia University Press · New York

Columbia University Press
Publishers Since 1893
New York   Chichester, West Sussex

Copyright © 2002 Columbia University Press
All rights reserved

Library of Congress Cataloging-in-Publication Data

Riess, Helen.
  Integrative group treatment for bulimia nervosa / Helen Riess and Mary Dockray-Miller.
     p. cm.
   includes bibliographical references.
   ISBN 0–231–12330–2 (cloth) —ISBN 0–231–12331–0 (paper)
     1. Bulimia—Treatment. 2. Eating disorders. I. Dockray-Miller, Mary, 1965– II. Title.

RC552.B84 R54 2001
616.85'2630651—dc21

2001037261

Columbia University Press books
are printed on permanent and durable acid-free paper.

∞

Printed in the United States of America
c 10 9 8 7 6 5 4 3 2 1
p 10 9 8 7 6 5 4 3 2 1

Designed and composed by Todd Duren of Firefly Design

Text is set in Granjon, and titles in Officina Serif

For Claire and Cordelia
our dancing daughters

Contents

Preface

Group therapy has been shown to be an effective method for treating bulimia nervosa (BN) for almost two decades. The types of group therapy range from long-term, open-ended, psychodynamic psychotherapy groups to time-limited cognitive behavioral therapy (CBT), as well as psychoeducational and experiential group treatments, to the newer applications of interpersonal therapy (IPT) and relational therapy (RT) offered in group settings. The twelve-session integrative group-therapy model described in this manual utilizes essential psychoeducational and cognitive behavioral techniques aimed at symptom reduction and combines them with experiential, interpersonal, and relational therapies to address causes that underlie the outward manifestations of BN.

Use of an integrative approach borrows effective techniques from a variety of well-documented sources. The use of a time-limited group treatment as a first step in the treatment of BN has been described in detail (Riess and Rutan 1992) and supports the use of short-term groups as an introduction to treatment of this multifaceted disorder. Recent research shows the impressive effectiveness of cognitive behavioral therapy for symptom management (Cooper, Coker, and Fleming 1996; Fairburn, Agras, and Wilson 1992; Schmidt and Treasure 1997; Spangler 1999; Thiels, Schmidt, Treasure, and Garthe 1998; Treasure et al. 1996; White 1999; Wilson 1999; Wilson et al. 1999; Wilfley and Cohen 1997). These studies focus on individual rather than group therapy, and the exclusive aim of the treatments is elimination of symptoms.

ix

Fairburn, Jones, Peveler, Hope, and O'Connor's 1993 study comparing longer-term effects of IPT, CBT, and behavioral therapy (BT) showed that IPT and CBT were much more effective than BT alone. While CBT was initially more effective in reducing bulimic episodes in the first eight months than IPT, at twelve-month-follow-up the two treatments were equally effective. This landmark study confirmed psychotherapists' widely held belief that once improved relational functioning is achieved, the need to express inner conflict by use of bulimic symptoms is diminished.

Recent reports utilizing IPT demonstrate decreasing bulimic symptoms by examining and mastering interpersonal skills in relationships (Apple 1999; Fairburn 1993; Fedele and Harrington 1990). By making connections between a bulimic woman's relationship with food and her relationships with herself and others, RT is an effective form of treatment in patients with eating disorders (Tantillo 1998; Steiner-Adair 1991; Surrey 1987). The effectiveness of experiential therapies—emphasizing guided imagery, structured eating, movement therapy, psychodrama, and experiencing the self—has been reported by Hornyak and Baker (1989).

This manual integrates key healing factors from the above therapies to provide a unique approach shown to be highly effective in reducing bulimic symptoms and in significantly decreasing scores on group members' Beck Depression Inventories. Experiencing an integrative treatment such as the one described here can help group members discern which specific treatment focus most closely matches their individual needs. Since BN is a chronic disorder characterized by remissions and relapses, group members are often at different stages with regard to symptom severity, insight into underlying causes, and capacity for relating to others. An integrative model can help members identify their immediate needs, as well as their ongoing needs for symptom monitoring, interpersonal and relational problem solving, or both, at the end of the group treatment.

The manual that follows describes in detail a twelve-session group treatment that has been offered at Massachusetts General Hospital in Boston, Massachusetts. Efficacy data for patients who met *DSM-IV* criteria for bulimia nervosa reveals significant improvement in frequency of bingeing and purging behaviors, as well as improvement in depression as measured by Beck Depression Inventory scores. (For detailed research results, see Riess 2002; see also the conclusion to this manual).

Eating disorders affect an estimated 5–19 percent of college women across the country in varying degrees of severity (Halmi 1981). Over the past decade, the age of affected females has dropped steadily to include high school– and junior high school–age girls. Traditionally, treatment for BN has been offered at hospitals and mental health facilities. While these locations should continue to offer such therapy, our experience with school populations suggests that every college and university health service, high school, and junior high school must be prepared to meet the needs of young women with BN. The introductory group treatment that follows is a methodical, integrative approach that has demonstrated effectiveness.

Integrative group treatment is an ideal entry point for eating disorder treatment, as it immediately addresses the distressing behaviors for which the individual is seeking help while diminishing feelings of isolation that come with the secretive nature of BN. It allows the member to obtain symptom control before addressing all of the underlying causes (Barth and Wurman 1986). Group therapy provides a setting where self-disclosure and risk-taking enable patients to learn how to be authentic in relation to others—first in the group, as they discover their conflicts and begin to heal emotional wounds, and eventually in their everyday lives. Group treatment offers a built-in opportunity to deal with interpersonal and inter-relational issues through group interactions and disclosures of personal conflicts and dilemmas that occur outside the group.

The treatment model that follows can be administered by a wide variety of health care professionals. These include social workers, university health service nurses or nurse practitioners, nurse clinical specialists in psychiatry, and psychologists, mental health workers, or psychiatrists. In the high-school setting, clinically trained counselors can provide this group treatment. The integrative group approach can also be offered in day hospital settings as well as after-care programs following discharge from inpatient settings. In the outpatient setting, we have used the groups as a training opportunity, by having a trainee serve as coleader with an experienced leader. Thus the number of groups offered can grow as more professionals become proficient in group technique.

With today's emphasis on cost containment in all aspects of medical care, the group approach is not only an affordable option but a way for each member to gauge specifically her need for a particular type of future treatment, if such treatment is indicated. Having exposure to CBT, RT, IPT, and psychoeducational techniques will enable members to choose specific forms of further treatment. Group members come away from this time-limited group with marked symptom reduction and a deeper appreciation of the underlying causes of their disorder. After acquiring the tools they need to manage their symptoms, many elect to continue work on improving self-esteem, assertiveness, self-growth, and self-understanding in subsequent treatments.

The objective in writing this group leaders' guide is to encourage practitioners treating eating disordered patients to offer this effective form of treatment. By reducing symptoms and enlightening patients about medical risks, nutritional information, practical ways to manage food intake, and underlying personal dynamics, leaders can enable group members to overcome their preoccupations with food as a substitute for effective and satisfying living. It is my hope that many women will be helped by this model and will find freedom from the debilitating confines of their battles with bulimia.

Helen Riess

Acknowledgments

Through a chance meeting at our daughters' ballet class, we discovered our common interest in girls, women's issues, and eating disorders. This manual is the result of weaving together the academic paths that each of us had taken before that meeting. Mary brought her interests in women's history and cultural studies to the project; Helen brought her clinical and research background in eating disorders. These complementary fields produced the following manual that can be used to treat the large number of women suffering from bulimia nervosa in contemporary culture.

Helen

I would like to thank my current and former colleagues in the Eating Disorders Unit at Massachusetts General Hospital for their support of this integrative group therapy program. They include Anne Becker, M.D., Ph.D.; Carol DoCouto, M.Ed., R.D.; Debra Franko, Ph.D.; Paul Hamburg, M.D.; David Herzog, M.D.; Rosalind Kearney, Ph.D.; Julia Reade, M.D.; Dale Sokoloff, Psy.D.; and Laura Weisberg, Ph.D. Special thanks to Ginger Chappell, Ph.D.; Judith Craver, Ph.D.; and Nancy Etcoff, Ph.D., for their careful reading of the manuscript and helpful comments. I am deeply indebted to Dr. Ned Cassem, who was chief of psychiatry at Massachusetts General Hospital. He provided untold encouragement for me in support of my interest in eating disorders

xiii

throughout the years and supported me in obtaining the Ethel Dupont-Warren Fellowship, which funded this research. Many thanks to Anne Alonso, Ph.D., and J. Scott Rutan, Ph.D., for teaching me the theory and practice of group psychotherapy and to Lee Cohen, M.D., for encouraging this project. Special thanks to John Herman, M.D., for creating the Web site for this manual. My enduring thanks to Johanna Thoeresz and Melissa Kraft for their resolute support of my interests and career from the beginning, and to Irene Briggin, M.D., for her wisdom. Finally, this book could not have been written without the courageous patients who entrusted their care to us and taught us so much about their struggles with nourishing themselves.

Mary

I would like to thank Lynn Janovsky of Grey Advertising for reports on popular culture; Cynthia Jirak of the Lesley University Counseling Service for advice about journals; and Janna Yamron, M.S., R.D., for reflection and consultation about eating disorders throughout the twentieth century. I would especially like to thank my undergraduate students in the Women's College at Lesley University, whose enthusiasm and curiosity in the classroom continually remind me of the importance of the battle against eating disorders in the lives of contemporary young women.

We would both like to thank John Michel, senior editor, and Godwin Chu, assistant manuscript editor, at Columbia University Press for their commitment to and help with this project. Finally, we thank our husbands, Norm Nishioka and Mike Miller, and our children, Grant and Claire, Cordelia and Bryn.

Acknowledgments

Integrative Group Treatment

for Bulimia Nervosa

Introduction

This manual is intended as a guide for trained professionals in a variety of settings where bulimia nervosa may be encountered, from hospital clinics to university health centers. The types of professionals who can provide this type of care include: social workers, certified counselors, nurse clinical specialists in psychiatry, nurses in university health settings, psychologists, psychiatrists, and mental health workers. This integrative group treatment model for bulimia nervosa is designed for six to ten participants meeting once a week with one or two group leaders for ninety minutes for twelve weeks. This manual will guide the leader in providing time-limited treatment for bulimia using psychoeducational and cognitive behavioral techniques, as well as interpersonal, experiential, and relational treatment strategies.

Overview

Eating disorders are but one of many specific pathological responses to the pressures of the modern world. Although anorexia nervosa and bulimia nervosa are not newly described syndromes, their frequent occurrence in today's young women suggests that our modern culture fosters and perpetuates these syndromes. An outbreak of anorexia nervosa in the late 1920s and early 1930s was short-lived (Beuf 1976). This coincided

1

with the first wave of women's emancipation from traditional sex roles, with slenderness representing nonreproductive sexuality and a form of androgynous independence (Bennett and Gurin 1982). Full-figured women were considered fashionable in the 1940s and 1950s, but a rise in eating disorders recurred in the late 1960s and early 1970s when fashion trends portrayed extremely thin models (such as Twiggy) as ideal (Beuf 1976). The challenges to traditional sex roles by the women's movement, as well as general cultural unrest indicative of American society since 1965, help to explain why anorexia and bulimia became so widespread in the late twentieth century. A number of cultural factors serve to foster these disorders. These include role confusion caused by the conflicted expectations of traditional femininity and success in what has traditionally been a man's world. In addition, the *anomie* of today's society could be leaving women anxious, isolated, and uncertain. Some young women seem to be literally "starving for love" in a world where others' self- preoccupation leaves them with little confidence in their own self-worth.

It is generally agreed upon that eating disorders arise from a combination of risk factors, including sociocultural issues, psychological susceptibility, biological vulnerabilities, and familial predispositions. The fact that our society historically has the highest number of reports of these disorders suggests that there is something idiosyncratic about our particular culture and time in history that increases the risk of eating disorders in modern women. The ever-growing number of young women suffering from self-starvation and deprivation makes it incumbent upon us to find therapeutic measures to treat and cure these all too pervasive disorders. Consideration of all these factors indicates that group therapy would provide support for such individuals' finding their own particular roles in society, a sense of connection to others, and a forum in which to explore each member's cultural and personal desires.

2

This introduction will provide a brief description of the historical roots of the disorder; the definition of bulimia nervosa, along with information about its epidemiology and etiology; and a rationale for the use of this time-limited group treatment for bulimia nervosa.

Historical Roots

Medical reports of anorexia nervosa date back to the seventeenth century (Morton 1694/1985), and bulimic symptoms have been described in the medical literature since the late nineteenth century. The first documented account of bulimia as a disorder in its own right, and not a symptom associated with other illnesses, was not published until the mid-twentieth century. The term "bulimarexia" was introduced in 1976 to describe the growing numbers of anorectic women who also binged (Boskind-Lodahl and White 1976). We have continued to see such a rise in the numbers of patients presenting with eating disorders, and it is estimated that from 5 to 10 percent of young women meet criteria for eating disorders (Pope, Hudson, and Yurgelun-Todd 1984). Some reports show that as many as 5 to 19 percent of female college students have the essential symptoms of bulimia nervosa (Halmi, Falk, and Schwartz 1981; Pyle, Mitchell, Hatsukami, and Goff 1984). These numbers are still valid (Becker, Grinspoon, Klibanski, and Herzog 1999).

Although eating disorders are not new, their incidence and prevalence are such that they cannot be overlooked in reports of psychiatric illness in our current culture. Clearly, we must examine why these disorders are so prevalent today, particularly when bulimia was scarcely recognized in the early part of the twentieth century and anorectic women were considered oddities of past centuries.

Brumberg (1988) maintains that self-starvation has had different meanings in different times and cultures. Medieval ascetics such as Catherine of Sienna were elevated to the rank of sainthood because of

3

their severe austerity and "miraculous" ability to fast. Women in the nineteenth century used not eating as their own form of control and protection from a society that thrust them into roles for which they were unprepared. Brumberg's point is that in the past two centuries "appetite became less of a biological drive and more a social and emotional instrument." Twentieth-century women with eating disorders are using this instrument to combat their own sense of role confusion, insecurity, and conflicting expectations that modern society and their female heritage dictate. Today thousands of young women are dedicated to fasting and dieting, but these behaviors are not seen as abnormal until drastic physiological or mental changes indicate that the dieter has gone overboard.

Modern women are obsessed with thinness. Were this not true, the diet industry with its weight-loss clinics, diet books, and exercise plans guaranteed to shed unwanted pounds would not be a multimillion-dollar business. Not everyone who embarks on a weight loss diet has an eating disorder, but the diet culture has contributed to the pervasive problem of eating disorders. The current emphasis on extremely slim figures provides modern women with an unattainable goal that is used to measure self-worth and self-love rather than simple body weight. If we consider the modern aphorism that "You can't be too rich or too thin," it is no surprise that so many young women dedicate themselves to lives of rigid self-control and the torture of thwarting their appetites in order to feel attractive and acceptable.

Definitions

Bulimia nervosa is characterized by binge eating followed by a number of different efforts to counteract the resultant weight gain (Russell 1979). The latest diagnostic criteria for bulimia nervosa as described in the *DSM-IV* are: recurrent episodes of binge eating (rapid consumption of a large amount of food in a discrete period of time); a feeling of lack of

4

control over eating behavior during eating binges; regular engagement in either self-induced vomiting, use of laxatives or diuretics, strict dieting or fasting, or vigorous exercise in order to prevent weight gain; a minimum average of two binge eating episodes a week for at least three months; a self-evaluation unduly influenced by body shape and weight; occurrence of the disturbance exclusive of episodes of anorexia nervosa (*DSM-IV*, 1994). These criteria have been most recently revised to distinguish the symptom (binge eating) from the diagnostic syndrome (bulimia nervosa). Both anorexia and bulimia nervosa are serious disorders that can place those afflicted at risk for sudden death. Anorectic women can literally starve to death, while bulimic women may lose vital electrolytes through purging behaviors that result in cardiac compromise. When the two disorders coexist in the same person, she is particularly at risk for serious medical complications. (For a critique of the *DSM-IV* criteria, see Hay and Fairburn 1998; Sullivan, Bulik, and Kendler 1998).

Epidemiology

Eating disorders predominantly afflict young women; 90–95 percent of the anorectic and bulimic populations are female. Original reports of eating disorders associated them with the upper-middle socioeconomic class (Garfinkle and Garner 1982), but current data indicate that they occur in all socioeconomic classes and major ethnic groups in the United States and are more prevalent internationally in industrialized societies than in nonindustrialized societies (Crago, Shisslak, and Estes 1996; Gard and Freeman 1996; Pike and Walsh 1996). The onset of anorexia tends to occur at an earlier age than bulimia. In anorexia the onset occurs between ages twelve to twenty-five, with a bimodal peak at ages fourteen and eighteen (Eckert 1985). Bulimia nervosa is primarily a disorder of young adult women, beginning between seventeen and twenty-five years of age (Halmi, Falk, and Schwartz 1981). Most bulimic women are

5

within a normal weight range, but as many as 50 percent have a history of being overweight (Johnson and Connors 1987). Cases of bulimia are much more difficult to detect because of the secretive nature of the disorder and the apparently normal physical appearance of the affected person.

Etiology

The etiology of the eating disorders involves an interplay of psychological, sociocultural, familial, and biological factors.

Psychological Factors

Psychoanalysts in the early history of treating eating disorders believed that self-starvation was a defense against sexual fantasies of oral impregnation or against ambivalent sadistic fantasies (Herzog 1988). Ego psychologists and object relations theorists maintained that eating disorders are a result of early defects in ego structure and object failures. They postulated that self-deficits originating from the lack of appropriate responses from the mother to the child lead to a sense of ineffectiveness, helplessness, and self-hatred. Hilde Bruch's landmark 1973 theory postulated that mothers who use feedings primarily to quiet the child rather than to respond to the child's hunger do not help the child to distinguish his or her own needs from those of others. When older, the child feels a connection with her mother by attending to the mother's wishes and needs rather than her own.

Such dynamics lead to an overwillingness to comply with others' wishes and a tendency to become overly perfectionistic in areas that appeal to parents, such as high scholastic achievement, athletic prowess, and development of other special skills. When a child turns to the pursuit of thinness as a way to achieve self-control and perfectionism, the distorted sense that she can never become thin enough leads to self-loathing, depression,

6

and low self-esteem. A feedback cycle is initiated whereby low self-esteem leads to extreme concerns about body image, which results in strict dieting that often leads to bingeing and purging, which then increases low self-esteem. See figure below.

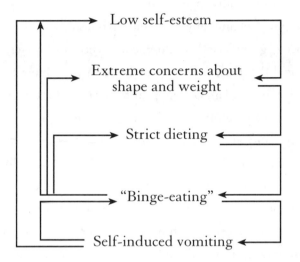

The cognitive-behavioral model of the maintenance of bulimia nervosa. From Fairburn, Marcus, and Wilson (1993, p. 369). Copyright 1993 by The Guilford Press. Reprinted by permission.

Increased conflicts can occur when high achievement and accomplishment threaten connections with peers. Today relational and interpersonal theorists focus on the lack of mutuality and inability to manage interpersonal conflicts in significant relationships as major contributors to womens' preoccupation with food and weight. By adopting societal values for autonomy and independence, women bury their needs for mutuality, self acceptance, and empowerment in a secret struggle with food. Binge eating can represent the overwhelming need to fill up an empty, inner void, while purging can signify an immediate rejection of those very needs by the act of undoing. By denying the need for psychological nurturing as well as the need for food, women construct an outward false self of independence and autonomy while denying their needs for empathy and connections to others. This double bind confines them in a destructive relationship with food rather than a relationship with supportive others.

The power of mutually empathic relationships for an overall sense of well-being, growth, and development has been extensively described by relational theorists, such as Jean Baker Miller, Janet Surrey, and Catherine Steiner-Adair. Girls appear to be at risk for disconnection as they mature in our culture. Their basic needs for connection characterized by mutuality are met with conflicts when they are faced with the high value placed on autonomy, competition, and high performance in our culture. This conflicts with their need for mutual connection with other girls and women. Mutuality in relationships is seen as critical to a woman's psychological growth because it increases knowledge about oneself, the other person, and a mutual appreciation of each others' self-worth and need for self-validation (Miller 1988).

The use of interpersonal interactions within a therapy group as the primary implement for change has been well described by Yalom (1985). Klerman et al. (1984) observed that the parts of the self that lead to maintenance of attachment are stimulated in significant relationships, and that those threatening attachment are selectively disavowed, resulting in lasting personality traits. The process of affect attunement between parents and child is a major mechanism conferring a child's sense that his or her emotional experience is human and shareable. Emotional attunement also conveys to the individual a sense of how he or she is appraised by others (Safron

8

and Segal 1990). Appraisal by others is a major component of womens' obsession with weight and food that promotes disordered eating. Fairburn (1993) modified IPT for patients with BN. The rationale was that binge eating occurred as a response to interpersonal disturbances (i.e., social isolation, fears of rejection and consequent negative moods). IPT assumes that the mastery of current social roles and adaptations to interpersonal situations are sufficient for treatment effectiveness because of the interrelationships between low self-esteem, negative mood, interpersonal functioning, and eating.

The relational approach to group therapy takes the interpersonal interaction to a more explicit level, focusing on the way in which a relationship with food takes the place of relationships with others. Fedele and Harrington (1990) have described four healing factors present in women's groups that promote healthy relationships: validation, self-empathy, mutuality, and empowerment. When these factors are encouraged in interpersonal relationships, the need to hide the self in a relationship with food (by binge eating and purging) diminishes, and the true expression of the self in relationship to others is empowered.

Sociocultural Factors

The present sociocultural milieu in western societies fosters the notion that physical attractiveness in women necessitates a slender, lean body. Although the recent fitness culture promotes exercise primarily for healthy bodies, an emphasis on slimness rather than muscle tone prevails for women. Magazine and television models continue to portray extremely thin bodies as the norm for today's women. The effect of these models is twofold: some women try to imitate them by rigorous exercise routines and dieting, while others feel inadequate and depressed that

9

they can never reach this thin ideal. Research by Becker et al. (2001) in an entirely different cultural setting, Fiji, demonstrated that Fijian women had no preoccupation with thinness until the advent of television in their society in 1995. Before that time, the Fijian aesthetic ideal was a robust female body. With the advent of television and exposure to extremely thin celebrities and models, Fijians experienced a dramatic increase in disordered eating. This cross-cultural research lends credence to the powerful influence that the media confer on women's self-image.

One of the effects of our male-dominated society is that women's perceptions of themselves are influenced by the way men see them (Wolf 1991; Boskind-Lodahl and White 1976). Young women learn that thin is desirable, and in an effort to be loved, held in high esteem, and taken care of, they will starve themselves or resort to bulimic behaviors to feel acceptable.

Familial Factors

More often than not, the patient with an eating disorder is a member of a dysfunctional or troubled family. The problems in the family are usually not spoken about and thus remain unresolved, so that the eating-disordered member becomes the targeted problem child. For example, when the threat of divorce is not verbalized, the child becomes symptomatic, and the family's energy is refocused on the child, thus keeping the parents together. Should the child recover, the threat of divorce resurfaces. As a result, the child becomes stuck in a static role, impairing her own development and warding off her own fears about maturation and sexuality.

The typical family of an eating-disordered patient is characterized by rigidity, overprotection, enmeshment, lack of conflict resolution, and the use of the child to mitigate parental conflicts (Minuchin, Rosman, and Baker 1978).

10

Biological Factors

Abnormalities of the hypothalamic-pituitary-adrenal axis appear in both depression and eating disorders (Doerr, Fichter, Pirke, and Lund 1980). Researchers of bulimia suggest that there may be a central neurochemical abnormality of the serotonergic and noradrenergic systems. Serotonin causes the sensation of satiety, and the low level of this neurotransmitter in bulimic women may predispose them to binging behaviors (Kaye, Ebert, Gwirtsman, and Weiss 1984). Further evidence of a biological component in the etiology of eating disorders is the ameliorating effect of the antidepressant medications that act on noradrenergic and serotonergic receptors. Research indicates that a combination of antidepressant medication and psychotherapy produces better results with bulimic women than with anorectic women (Peterson and Mitchell 1999).

Treatments

Treatment of eating disorders can be difficult and problematic because of the coexisting, multiaxial etiologies and the functional severity of the symptomatology. Several promising treatment modalities have emerged, but no single treatment has been shown to be universally effective. Inpatient treatment is usually reserved for medically unstable patients, suicidal patients, or those whose family situations are so destructive that temporary separation from the family is necessary. Among the outpatient treatments that have been reported to be useful, alone or in combination, are individual psychotherapy (psychodynamic, cognitive-behavioral, behavioral), family therapy, nutritional therapy, pharmacotherapy, and group psychotherapy.

Group therapy addresses the four etiologies of eating disorders: teaching the sociocultural context, discussing both the psychological and familial constellation of each member, and providing a forum to address

11

the biological etiology by discussing the benefits of or disappointments in medications. Group therapy has emerged as a favored treatment for patients with bulimia nervosa (Brotman, Alonso, and Herzog 1986). Furthermore, there are many types of group therapy available for eating disordered patients. Deciding which type of group to recommend for patients is difficult because many different forms are touted to be effective. Time-limited psychoeducational groups and cognitive-behavioral groups have received wide acclaim for results in decreasing bulimic symptoms, while open-ended psychodynamically oriented groups are reported to repair the gaps in ego structure necessary for long lasting recovery (Barth and Wurman 1986; Browning 1985; Cooper, Coker, and Fleming 1996; Spangler 1999; Thiels, Schmidt, Treasure, and Garthe 1998; Treasure et al. 1996; White 1999; Wilfley 1997; Wilson 1999; Wilson et al. 1999). Recently, interpersonal and relational therapy groups have been reported to be effective for BN (Apple 1999; Tantillo 1998).

Although the literature is replete with reports of success using time-limited cognitive-behavioral groups and psychoeducational groups, the lack of long-term follow-up studies makes it difficult to determine how lasting the reported decreases in symptomatology will be. Although bulimic symptoms such as binge eating and purging are easy to measure, and weight gain or loss in the anorectic woman can be a concrete sign of progress or relapse, it is far more difficult to measure the extent to which the underlying psychopathology has been diagnosed and treated. The chronic nature of anorexia and bulimia nervosa, with their frequent relapses during periods of stress, suggest that underlying gaps in ego structure must be addressed and corrected before complete healing can occur. Such goals can be accomplished in long-term, open-ended psychotherapy groups or in individual psychotherapy.

Group therapy provides eating disordered patients with a safe environment to disclose and discuss their illness—usually a well-guarded secret shrouded in shame, guilt, and self-hatred. The isolation that develops around this disorder can be profound: Bulimic patients often have symptoms for five to ten years before seeking help (Herzog 1988). Group treatments help patients explore their inner experiences and their interpersonal relationships by functioning as a paradigm for relationships in the outside world. Group therapy also helps patients examine the potential relationship between family dynamics and their eating disorders. As the group process develops, patients learn to appreciate the unique role that their eating symptoms served for themselves as individuals as well as for their families (Brotman, Alonso, and Herzog 1986).

While open-ended psychodynamically oriented groups for eating disordered patients are ideal for exploring the underlying individual and familial contexts in which eating disoders have developed, they are typically difficult to form. Patients are often at different levels with regard to symptom management, and the lack of focus on symptoms is frequently cited as a reason for early drop-outs. It is also difficult to introduce new members into long-term groups because long-term members find it difficult to focus on new members' preoccupation with symptoms once they have moved beyond their symptoms to the deeper underlying causes. In contrast, time-limited groups are not difficult to form. Reports of time-limited groups in the literature demonstrate this fact (Connors, Johnson, and Stuckey 1984; Kirkley, Schneidler, Agras, and Bachman 1985; Lacey 1983; Schneider and Agras 1985; Stevens and Salisbury 1984; Wolchik, Weiss, and Katzman 1986). Time-limited groups represent a limited commitment by members and immediately address the control of symptoms for which most patients are seeking help. In our experience at Massachusetts General Hospital, there have been far fewer drop-outs from time-limited groups, whereas it can take nine months to a year to form a stable core of members for an open-ended group. Time-limited treatment, then, can be used as an introduction to treatment with a focus on symptom management; it offers a screening device, an educational tool, and a demystification for open-ended dynamic group therapy, while also providing immediate attention to the reduction of bulimic symptoms.

The high acceptance rate for short-term treatments may reflect several factors: a clear beginning and end, focus on symptom reduction, a sense that less commitment is less risky, and lower cost in terms of time and money. In addition, a time-limited program makes successful completion more likely for the patient. About halfway through the highly structured groups, most members begin to feel comfortable enough to express feelings, to share personal experiences, and to sense that their eating symptoms have a great deal to do with their inner lives. It appears that the initial nonthreatening nature of the time-limited group enables members to bond around food issues and develop enough group safety to allow deeper aspects of themselves to emerge.

The manual that follows provides instructions for leading a time-limited therapy group for bulimic patients. A discussion of screening procedures for prospective members and a guide for processing group dynamics precede a step-by-step description of the twelve structured sessions. The integrative group approach has three phases, roughly divided between a psychoeducational component, a goal-oriented cognitive-behavioral component, and an interpersonal/relational component. These phases overlap and coexist rather than occupy discreet segments of the group experience. The experiential component is offered in the relaxation/visual imagery exercise (session seven) and the group meal (session ten).

Psychoeducational Phase
The psychoeducational phase is based on the assumption that lack of information and misconceptions about factors that cause and maintain symptoms are often present in patients with BN. Psychoeducation was originally pro-

14

posed as one component of treatment for both anorexia nervosa (AN) and BN by Garner, Rockert, Olmsted, Johnson, and Coscina (1985). The educational approach operates on the assumption that the patient is taking responsibility as a collaborative partner in her recovery, and that scientific information about factors perpetuating the disorder will increase motivation to discontinue symptoms. The educational principles are consistent with the overall didactic goals of CBT. There is evidence that brief treatments that are educationally oriented can lead to significant behavioral change in some patients (Ordman and Kirshenbaum 1986; Olmstead, Davis, Garner, Rockert, Irvine, and Eagle 1991).

The psychoeducational phase comprises the first three sessions of this integrative group model, where didactic information is verbally disseminated. Groups begin by having members introduce themselves and say a few words about what they hope to gain from being a member of the group. Group cohesion is fostered by initially focusing on external factors from our culture and society that foster eating disorders. The insidious and blatant pressures that the media convey to create anxiety and insecurities in women about their bodies are discussed. The focus on outside pressures brings the group together as a cohort upon which cultural and societal forces have operated. Many patients fear they are alone with their symptoms and that no one will understand them. Coming to a group represents a major step in breaking the silence about their bulimia and the fear and shame that accompanies disclosure. By shifting the focus to external factors, the group members realize that they are not entirely responsible for their preoccupation with food and weight, and this reduces the self-blame and self-hatred they often bring to group therapy. Knowing they are not alone with their eating disorder is an initial step in forming a powerful mutual bond with other group members.

The second session in the psychoeducational phase introduces a discussion of the medical consequences of BN, and the third addresses nutritional issues in patients with BN. Group cohesion is further established in two ways. By facing the medical sequelae the group is brought together by concern about the physically harmful aspects of BN. This shift in focus from outside pressures to the consequences their symptoms have on their physical well-being calls forth a sense of responsibility that each member has for the care of her body. The seriousness of the disorder and its ramifications tend to motivate and inspire members to change and encourage one another to do the same.

The nutrition session brings the group together around a shared hope that change is possible, and that nourishing the body does not equal weight gain and body dissatisfaction. This session introduces the concept that small, incremental changes are the way to recovery. This approach challenges the "all or none" thinking that many patients exhibit and is far less threatening than group members anticipate change to be. Conceptualizing food as nourishment that the body needs and deserves rather than as an enemy that has designs to make them fat helps to reframe the purpose of food and eating.

Cognitive Behavioral Phase

Although self-monitoring by keeping a written record of all eating behavior (a key component of CBT for BN) is introduced in session one, the CBT component begins more formally in the middle phase with weekly goal setting and other strategies. There are now many studies in the eating disorders literature reporting the efficacy of CBT for BN (see preface for a brief discussion). The following CBT techniques, developed by Fairburn and colleagues (Fairburn 1981, 1985; Fairburn, Marcus, and Wilson 1993), are utilized in this phase of the integrative group treatment:

Careful self-monitoring of all food intake as close to the time of consumption as possible. Food records provide the foundation for effective CBT, as they provide therapists with details of the eating problem (such as the circumstances and moods

16

surrounding the behavior). By helping to identify what is eaten and how symptoms are triggered, patients are able to increase control over their behavior. A sample food log follows the description of the first session, as well as a completed food log with examples of group leader's comments.

Identification of each eating episode as a meal, snack, or binge and whether the eating episode led to a binge.

Self-monitoring of all purging episodes, as well as the thoughts and feelings associated with each of these episodes.

Weighing no more than once a week. Daily use of scales encourages patients to gauge their mood, self-esteem, and self-value on a number rather than more complex assessments about the needs of the self as a whole.

Establishment of regular eating patterns. Restrictive dieting and skipping meals is common in BN. A first step in reducing bingeing and purging is planning three meals per day plus two snacks, because deprivation of food leads to binge eating. Eating small meals and planned snacks between meals is a first step toward regular eating patterns. Patients are also taught to distinguish "feeling fat" from "feeling full."

Strategies for self-control include planning specific places to eat at specific times, avoiding eating while driving or doing errands, eliminating availability of trigger foods, and structuring activities, such as taking a walk or meeting a friend, that can take the individual away from potential binge situations.

Cognitive restructuring aimed at correcting errors in reasoning and underlying erroneous assumptions that maintain disordered eating. An example of this is: "I can not socialize with my friends until I lose five pounds because no one will like me at this weight." Once this comment is made, the therapists can

17

challenge the assumption and remind the member that socializing with friends is what helps relieve the loneliness and anxiety that often leads to a night of binge eating.

Relapse prevention is a major goal of CBT. Recognizing that stressful times may result in recurrence of eating problems, and that a past history of BN may make patients vulnerable to using food as a coping mechanism helps them understand that setbacks may occur. Taking group members through an exercise in which they visualize themselves wearing a swim suit on an upcoming vacation, attending a party, or reacting to postpartum weight gain can help them identify triggers that may set off the desire to diet. Relapse prevention involves asking questions about consequences of using restrictive dieting and remembering the difficulties that ensued in the past when dieting was implemented to improve self-esteem.

Interpersonal/Relational Phase

"For women, mutually empathic relationships are essential for a sense of overall well-being and for promoting healthy growth and development. Such relationships are constructed through mutual understanding, emotional support, and the commitment of all individuals involved to the development of each individual and the collective unit."

(Surrey 1991, p. 246)

IPT was developed by Klerman et al. (1984) as a short-term focal psychotherapy for treatment of depression. It was found that since interpersonal difficulties contribute to the onset and maintenance of depression, resolving the conflicts would lead to recovery. Fairburn et al. (1991) modified IPT for patients with BN, and Wilfley et al. (1993) adapted

18

the Fairburn et al. (1991) approach to be used in a group format. The rationale for using IPT was that binge eating was a response to interpersonal disturbances, such as social isolation or fears of rejection and their consequent negative moods (Wilfley et al. 1993).

Klerman et al. described four main interpersonal problem areas: grief, interpersonal disputes, role transitions, and interpersonal deficits. IPT assumes that mastery of current social roles and adaptations to interpersonal situations are sufficient for treatment effectiveness because of the interrelationships between negative mood, low self-esteem, interpersonal functioning, and eating behavior (Fairburn et al. 1991). Use of an IPT group format is particularly suitable in the final third of integrative group treatment because relationships between group members are more defined by the eighth week.

The group leaders' responsibility in the relational phase of treatment is to emphasize the centrality of peer interactions in the social microcosm of the group. By using examples of the "here and now" of group process to facilitate mutuality in relationships, they clarify the process of change and demystify the notion that the power and answers lie with the group leaders (Grunebaum and Solomon 1982). The leaders accomplish the task of empowering relationships through greater emphasis on members' relationships with food and relationships with self and others by promoting the four healing factors found to be the most significant for women (Fedele and Harrington 1990): validation, self-empathy, mutuality, and empowerment. In the third phase of the group, leaders encourage members to relate specific examples of interpersonal conflicts, as they typically are relevant to the entire group. Interpersonal therapy for BN addresses members' problems with conflict avoidance, role expectation, regulation of needs of interpersonal closeness and distance, and lack of problem-solving skills in social situations (Apple 1999). The fundamental goals of relational therapy contribute to members' identifying

19

and then changing patterns that have kept them connected to food rather than to themselves and others (Tantillo 1998).

Sections discussing member screening and general guidance for group leaders follow this introduction. A conclusion suggesting areas for further research follows the description of the final session.

Screening Prospective Members for the Group

The importance of a thorough initial screening and intake of each group member cannot be overemphasized. Group-therapy literature reports that the more similarity that exists among members, the greater the likelihood that group cohesion will occur. Brotman et al. (1986) encourage a reasonably homogeneous level of object relations and symptomatology in group composition. Such cohesion best occurs when individuals feel they can relate well and empathize with other members. The most successful groups are those where the members are closely matched for age, gender, length of illness, and similarity of symptoms. Patients need to be on a similar level of psychological maturity in order to participate in a group. Careful screening also must ensure that the following conditions are met:

1. Members should meet the *DSM-IV* criteria for bulimia nervosa or clinically significant variants of a primary diagnosis of bulimia nervosa
2. Patients with a primary diagnosis of anorexia nervosa should be excluded

21

3. Patients with severe personality or psychotic disorders should be excluded

4. Actively suicidal patients should be excluded

5. Patients actively abusing alcohol or other chemical substances should be excluded

Discussion of These Conditions

1. Bulimia nervosa is the primary diagnosis. Clinically significant variants of BN should be included. Some individuals do not meet strict criteria (they may have symptoms less often than two times per week for three months), but they can still benefit from group treatment if their symptom profiles and thoughts about food match the other diagnostic criteria. These patients have shown significant improvement from the group experience, but should not be included in research outcome data. The *DSM-IV* criteria for the diagnosis of bulimia nervosa are:

1. Recurrent episodes of binge eating (rapid consumption of a large amount of food in a discrete period of time)

2. A feeling of lack of control over eating behavior during the eating binges

3. Regular engagement in either self-induced vomiting, use of laxatives or diuretics, strict dieting or fasting, or vigorous exercise in order to prevent weight gain

4. A minimum average of two binge eating episodes a week for at least three months

5. A self-evaluation unduly influenced by body shape and weight

6. Occurrence of the disturbance separate from episodes of anorexia nervosa

(*DSM-IV* 1994)

22

It is important to determine whether or not each prospective member meets these criteria since eating disorders cover a wide spectrum of behaviors. The structure of group therapy implies that all members are suffering from the same set of symptoms. Including individuals who only binge-eat without purging, for example, mixes populations and may make members feel they have less in common with one another. Members who were hoping that all participants had the same array of symptoms may feel less safe about disclosing their behaviors. The shame that accompanies purging behavior can be so profound that it must be an important, common problem addressed by the entire group.

   2. Patients with a primary diagnosis of anorexia nervosa should be excluded. The exclusion of patients with strict anorexia nervosa is necessary for several reasons. Anorexia has an earlier onset, affecting girls around the age of puberty, in the early teens. Anorectic patients typically have significant denial about their illness, have distorted body image, are at least 15 percent below expected body weight for height, and are usually sexually inexperienced and socially avoidant. Bulimic patients, in contrast, have symptoms usually starting in the late teen years, deny to others that they have symptoms (but are not in denial about their illness to themselves), and lack the degree of distortion in body perception found in anorectic patients. They are about normal weight for height, are usually sexually and socially experienced, and care a great deal about others' opinions. The presence of an anorectic woman in a therapy group for bulimic individuals can create a competitive environment in which the members with bulimia may experience themselves as "failed anorectics," looking at the thin girl's body as an ideal to strive for. The bulimic women may then tend to focus on looking like the anorectic group member rather than exploring the low self-esteem and depression that contribute to their own symptoms. Therefore, group cohesion can be seriously compromised by the presence of a member who

23

is entirely focused on food restriction rather than contributing to the group goal of changing purging and binge eating behaviors.

It is not always possible to determine the extent of underlying anorexia when forming a group. In one atypical case, a thin young woman came for an intake appointment complaining of binge eating and purging with laxatives. It became apparent from her food logs that her "binges" consisted of five saltine crackers followed by large quantities of laxatives. Since she had emphasized laxative abuse and addiction in the screening interview, we assessed her as having bulimia with anorexic tendencies and admitted her to the group. Socially, she was quite different from the other women, offering nothing in terms of self-disclosure and remaining very withdrawn. The group tried to engage her, but eventually group cohesion occurred around her rather than with her. The group leaders doubted that she was benefiting from the group at all until we noticed that her laxative use was diminishing significantly, as reported in her food log. At the last meeting, when all the members spoke about what they had found most useful in the group, she reported that she did not get anything out of the group except the knowledge that laxatives did not cause calorie reduction but only water loss. Her ability to make such an enormous change while appearing so disconnected from the group made us realize that the educational component of the group can have a powerful effect. Since she did not interfere with group process, as reported by Weiss and Katzman (1984), the group cohered in spite of her differences and allowed her to take from the group what she could at the time. Most often, however, an anorectic patient will tend to have a greater negative effect on group process.

3. Patients with severe personality or psychotic disorders should be excluded. While many bulimic women have elements of mixed histrionic, narcissistic, and borderline traits, a person who has full-blown borderline personality disorder as a primary diagnosis may harm the group and derive little

24

benefit from it. Such patients may not be able to relate to others and may find a group to be a ready opportunity for splitting and acting out. Such behavior can lead to group destruction, as the group may focus on rescuing this individual or on expunging her from the group. In persons with a severe personality or psychotic disorder, the eating behaviors may in fact require less focus, while intrapsychic stability and safety require the major focus of their treatment. Once patients are stabilized, a referral to an eating disorders group can be made at a later time.

4. Actively suicidal patients should be excluded. Actively suicidal patients, or patients who have recently made an attempt or who have been hospitalized for such an attempt, are too fragile for this kind of group. The group process encourages openness, trust, and commitment to change. Patients struggling with issues about whether life is worth living are asking questions vastly different from those women who are wondering if they can dare call a friend and go for a walk instead of staying home and binge eating. In one group, a woman, who had appeared healthier than she actually was at intake, had recently been discharged from an inpatient hospitalization. She became actively suicidal in the group and announced that she was much worse off than others in the group, that she felt helpless to make changes the way the others had, and that she was planning on taking all of her medication as soon as she got home. The group leaders ultimately had to call hospital security to take her to the emergency room. Alarm, guilt, and anger erupted in the group because of this incident, derailing the group's objectives for the next few sessions. The group members were eventually able to use their reactions to this emergency as a way of knowing and expressing their feelings about a shared experience. Such a disruption, although it can be worked with, would be better avoided; suicidal patients should be referred to long-term groups for stabilization, thus reserving time-limited eating disorder groups for less fragile patients.

25

5. Patients actively abusing alcohol or other chemical substances should be excluded. Patients with active alcoholism or substance abuse problems should be referred to substance abuse programs. It is too difficult for a patient to try to change eating symptoms when chemically addicted. Patients with diagnoses of active alcoholism and/or substance abuse are usually set up to fail if referred to a group with expectations for change in a food addiction while they are addicted to other substances. We have had patients who have minimized their alcohol consumption during screening interviews only to decompensate into debilitating chemical use because they were unable to make the same kinds of changes as their fellow members. Since binge and purge cycles serve as a defense against depression, low self-esteem, anxiety, and social incompetence, substance abusers may in fact increase drinking to ward off the intolerable feelings that emerge from binge or purge reduction. Such patients, who were sober when the group began, can have difficulty maintaining that sobriety as the group progresses because they cannot bear the feelings that may surface. Some members have consumed alcohol prior to group meetings to quell their anxieties. In such a situation, we have used group time to remind members of the difficulty of addressing more than one addiction at a time. We have tried to reinforce the member's desire for change (manifested by her joining the group at the outset) but have recommended that she center her goals on the chemical dependency (i.e., coming to group meeting sober) rather than the eating disordered symptoms. Although the group as a whole has seemed not to suffer negatively from a member who has presented this way, it has been quite difficult for such a member to bear the shame of failure. We encourage making every attempt to refer chemically dependent individuals to therapy to overcome chemical abuse prior to attempting therapy for an eating disorder.

Special Considerations

for Group Leaders

A Note About Group Dynamics

The following general notes about group dynamics may help leaders be aware of possible difficult situations before they arise.

Initially, the primary concern of every member who joins a therapy group is survival. A member's thoughts center on her psychological safety in the group; she wonders whether she can survive the potential threats to her psychic self. Most new members fear experiencing shame, humiliation, domination, and blame upon joining a group (Rutan, Alonso, and Groves 1988). Members are initially keenly aware of the leader's personality and style; all their senses are tuned in to whether the leader is safe, empathetic, and sustaining, or an untrustworthy and unpredictable figure (Levenkron 1978). The group leader must establish the safety of the group for the group to exist at all. Establishing an atmosphere of warmth, acceptance, and non-judgmental helpfulness is essential to the therapeutic encounter. Leaders must convey a genuine sense of wanting to help the members in their recoveries from bulimia through firmly establishing the group contract (see session one). An overview of what members can expect from the group is essential to their preparation for self-disclosure (such as keeping food records,

27

setting goals, and participating in the group meal), so they are not taken by surprise by the expectations of group procedure.

While group safety is the initial primary concern, other group dynamics tend to surface, and leaders should be aware of and anticipate these dynamics. Groups of young women with eating disorders can be highly competitive with each other in a variety of ways—for the attention of the group leader, for status as the thinnest or most articulate member of the group, or for recognition of a specific individual trait. If a particular group member is identified and silently assigned an idealized role by the group, that member may unconsciously accept the role of idealized person for the group, thereby abandoning her own needs in the service of meeting the needs of others.

It is not uncommon for a group member to be given the role of "junior therapist," turning the group experience into helping others rather than helping herself. This dynamic stems from the need to meet others' needs in order to feel valued as a person (see discussion of the false self in session eight). Group leaders must be able to identify this phenomenon and help the member who is being set up in this way to express her own needs and feelings. The group experience should be helpful to every member's recovery; it should not reinforce the notion that some members do not need very much and are there primarily to help the others (an all-too-familiar dynamic in the families of many eating-disordered women).

Competition for the love and attention of the leader can occur on many different levels. Some members compliment leaders on their skill or insights, while others bring in articles about eating disorders. Finely attuned management is required to acknowledge such manifestations in a respectful way that does not elevate one member over the others but appreciates the expression of good will. If a member brings an article to the leader, the member can be encouraged to share it with the group or

28

to make copies for the group, so that benefiting the group rather than pleasing the leader is reinforced. Compliments to the leader for insights and perceptions should be handled in a straightforward way, such as saying, "Thank you—it is important to know that you found that suggestion helpful," before moving on to cover other material (rather than opening the field for more focus on the leader). Unlike an open-ended psychotherapy group, the time-limited cognitive-behavioral approach does not explore the members' transference to the leader (i.e., the members' transferring their feelings about significant people in their lives onto the leaders).

Idealization is not the only feeling expressed toward group leaders. At times, a member can feel and express envy and anger at leaders who seem to have their lives and eating behaviors in order. It is not uncommon for members with more primitive defenses to "take a swipe" at the leader to throw her off guard and to see how the leader handles a situation she has not anticipated. Some members will ask how leaders stay so thin, or whether they are in recovery from eating disorders. These comments should be handled in a straightforward, nonexploratory manner. Unlike an open-ended psychotherapy group, where such inquiries may be used as a spring board for group process, this time-limited approach does not open up these types of discussions. It is important not to show annoyance or anger at such comments, but to treat them matter-of-factly and then move on to discussions that benefit the whole group. Statements, such as "Let's focus back on what we need to cover as a group today, so we can get to all the items on our agenda," will show the group member that this group has an objective that will not be derailed by such comments.

When two co-therapists lead a group, it is natural that some members will feel a greater affinity toward one leader than the other. Usually, this subtle favoritism does not present much of a problem. However, some

29

group members prone to using the defense of splitting may try to split the leaders into a "good" leader and a "bad" leader. These members praise whatever one leader says and challenge whatever the other leader says. The leaders must be prepared in advance for this type of splitting behavior, so that when it does happen, they are prepared to manage it in the group and to talk about it outside of group meetings. One way to minimize splitting is to refrain from playing it out. By referring to what the other leader has just said, for instance, demonstrates that there is no need for one leader to dominate the other leader. Preparation for this sort of dynamic will keep one therapist from feeling overvalued and the other devalued. Taking turns beginning each group meeting helps to establish parity between leaders, so that one is not viewed as the "main" leader and the other as the "secondary" leader.

Finally, leaders must be aware of and help to prevent the dynamic wherein one group member becomes the scapegoat for all of the group's unwanted feelings of inferiority, badness, helplessness, and hopelessness. If the group is comprised of members who are very closely matched for psychological developmental levels, this process usually does not happen in a cognitive-behaviorally oriented group. However, it is not always possible to determine the degree of psychopathology from an initial screening. In some groups, one member is at a markedly different developmental level from the others, and she can easily become the one member who is not taken seriously because her comments or goals do not match those of the others. It is important that the leaders take her seriously, not dismissing her comments with the implication that they are not worth listening to.

For example, in one group members were asked what they liked about their appearances. For one group member, the only thing she could think of that she liked was her feet. Some members of the group laughed and were ready to gloss over this statement and move on to members who could talk about more visible aspects of their appearance. The leaders intervened and asked the member to specify want she liked about her feet. This intervention made the member feel that her comment had value, and she continued, "My feet are the only perfect thing about me. They have no blemishes, no fat, the skin is smooth and soft. My feet are the only part of me that has never been criticized." This comment brought the entire group to silence at first, and then they all felt more emotionally connected to her. The rich discussion that followed centered on how they had come to love parts of themselves that others loved, but also on how they had stopped viewing themselves as whole people and saw themselves only as fragmented parts, each with a judgment attached (good feet, good hair, bad skin, bad thighs). The need to stop this fragmentation became apparent only after this member had shared her feelings about her feet. After this session, the other members viewed her differently, and she was given the same degree of respect as the other members of the group.

A Note About the Curriculum Readings

Leaders should be aware that the essays included as curriculum readings can be supplemented or changed by leaders with specific considerations (such as the particular age of the group's population). Topical and timely articles from a number of publications in popular culture can provide current information about eating disorders that may be especially relevant to a particular group and can take the place of some of the essays in this manual. We have also found it helpful to bring to meetings examples of current magazine advertisements to illustrate the powerful messages about body image that the media convey to their readers. Leaders may also encourage group members to bring in such examples that are particularly striking to them.

31

A Brief Outline of
Twelve Sessions

Psychoeducational Phase

Session one introduces the group leader(s) and members to one another. It establishes the group contract, presents a historical overview of perceptions and presentations of women's body shape, and introduces set-point theory as a medical reason for weight-loss diet failure. The group leader(s) issues food logs to members with instructions for their use, and assigns the essay "The Diet Conspiracy."

Session two includes discussion of the essay assigned last session. Its main focus is instruction in the medical complications of eating disorders. Group leaders need to ensure that members understand the long-term physiological consequences of their disorder. Finally, leaders broach the subject of forming new eating habits and provide a forum for continuing the work of keeping a food log. This session is highly didactic, like the previous one, but provides opportunity for personal reflection and discussion as the members begin to feel comfortable with one another and with the group leader(s). The handout "Physical Manifestations of Bulimia Nervosa" is distributed.

33

Session three presents a model of balanced nutrition to group members through a lecture and discussion about healthy eating habits. That model is then put into practice, to some extent, when the food log sheets from the previous week are returned to individual members with comments from the leader (see example on page 38). This session illustrates that each group member may struggle with different aspects of the illness, but that basic tenets of healthy eating must be learned and gradually incorporated into a person's behavior in order to regulate her eating patterns. The essay "Two Raisinets and a Cornflake" is assigned at the end of the meeting.

Cognitive Behavioral Phase

Session four begins the members' active participation in and commitment to group therapy. In the first three sessions members largely listened and learned; now they begin to analyze and modify their behaviors through goal-setting strategies. After discussing the assigned reading, the members set goals that are short-term, positive, reasonable, and specific; these goals are designed after examination of the three completed food logs. All of the remaining sessions include segments on goals and food logs, providing a sense of continuity and routine for the group.

Session five focuses on strategies for coping with emotionally stressful situations. The group suggests a list of preventive strategies for both general and specific situations (being alone in the evening, for example, or visiting with relatives over the holidays). The leader introduces the concept of reframing "failure" as a learning experience. The session ends with segments on goals and food logs. The handout "Strategies and Suggestions to Prevent Binge Eating" is distributed.

Session six is composed mainly of a discussion and analysis of the function served in members' lives by bingeing and purging. Members thus envision their lives without bingeing and purging, using psychodramatic role playing as a tool to facilitate discussion. Since the group is now

34

at its halfway point, members are more comfortable with each other, the group has coalesced, and open discussions have gradually become a larger part of each session. The session ends with goals and food logs.

Session seven provides opportunity for members to discuss behavior chains and members' goals for breaking those chains. Behavior chains are a series of linked behaviors that have automatically resulted in binge eating and purging. The behavior chain exercise is tied to food logs and goal setting; the group sets goals and turns in the food logs prior to the relaxation exercise that follows. Next, discussion touches upon the relationship between anxiety and bulimia (bingeing and purging usually serve as anxiety relievers). The group then participates in an experiential therapy technique, using visual imagery to achieve relaxation as an alternative to bingeing and purging. The group actively participates in a relaxation exercise led by the group leader, tensing and releasing muscles, using visual imagery to achieve a relaxed state, envisioning a relaxing place, and controlling breathing. The essay "Celebrating Achievement" is assigned for next week.

Interpersonal/Relational Phase

Session eight focuses on interpersonal interactions between members and their significant others. The role of assertiveness and conflict resolution is introduced. Patients discuss the differences between assertiveness and aggressiveness; leaders set up role-playing exercises to model assertive behavior in conflict-laden situations. The concepts of self-empathy, validation, mutuality, and empowerment are introduced. Leaders solicit situations and examples from members' lives to provide immediate relevance for the role-playing exercise. Leaders solicit reactions to the essay "Celebrating Achievement" before segments on goals and food logs. Leaders inform members that there will be a group meal in session ten, which will be discussed and planned in session nine; they assign the essay "Nourishing the Self" for next time.

Session nine focuses on the ability to recognize and express feelings verbally (rather than with food). This session challenges the unconscious motivations that lead individuals to choose a relationship with food rather than a closer relationship to others. Examination of the "mood" column in the food logs leads to recognition of connections between binge/purge behaviors and certain emotions. Members realize that they are using food to avoid recognition of feelings. Referring to the assigned essay, "Nourishing the Self," leaders encourage discussion about feelings of neediness, deprivation, rejection, sadness, anxiety, and anger; leaders emphasize the importance of being able to recognize and feel these emotions. Very often the negative feelings that are being warded off by preoccupation with food are identified as sadness and anger regarding the lack of mutuality in their significant relationships. The group sets final plans for the group meal (next session), and the session ends with goal setting and food logs.

Session ten is the group meal, an experiential exercise that includes structured eating and experiencing the self in the actual setting in which eating conflicts occur. The session begins with a discussion of the rationale for the group meal. The group explores each member's feelings before, during, and after the meal. This session also represents an exposure-and-response prevention exercise; since the automatic response of purging is not an option, members must sit with the feelings of fullness after the meal. Members are required to remain in the group room until the end of the session. The session ends with goals and food logs.

Session eleven begins the process of ending the group. Discussion of last week's session evolves into a discussion of feelings about the group's termination. Leaders present options for continued treatment after termination, meeting briefly with each individual to discuss her needs. The group leader(s) assigns the essay "Breaking Down the Prison Walls" for next session. The session ends with goal setting and food logs.

36

Session twelve closes the group cycle with open discussion about members' experience in and reaction to the group, evaluation of the group, and information about contacting leaders for future care and referrals. Segments on goals and food logs; encouragement to use group therapy strategies (relaxation, assertiveness, prevention, goal setting), even when not in therapy. Discussion of the essay "Breaking Down the Prison Walls" ends the group cycle on a note of hopefulness, recovery, and optimism. The last session ends with goal setting and food logs.

See p. 38 for a sample food log, which is distributed to each member every week, and p. 39 for a sample of a completed food log with comments written by the group leader. The sample food log and assigned readings can also be downloaded online at http://www.massgeneral.org/allpsych/.

FOOD LOG

Date	Time	Breakfast, Lunch, Dinner, Snack, Binge	Who is present?	Mood	Food Consumed	Purge? Vomiting, Laxatives, Diuretics, etc.	Mood After Eating

This sample food log can be reproduced and enlarged on a copy machine. It can also be downloaded online at http://www.massgeneral.org/allpsych/.

FOOD LOG — Sample Patient Log with Leader's Comments (shaded)

Date	Time	Breakfast, Lunch, Dinner, Snack, Binge	Who is present?	Mood	Food Consumed	Purge? Vomiting, Laxatives, Diuretics, etc.	Mood After Eating
Thurs 12	8:30	Breakfast	Myself	Restless	1/2 grapefruit *Having no protein to satisfy your hunger is a set up for a binge later in day.*	No	Hungry
	12:30	Lunch	Friend Jane	Cold, tired, irritable	green salad, low fat dressing, cup of tea	No	Irritated
	4:30	Snack	Myself	Hungry & cold	tea with skim milk		
	6:45	Dinner→Binge	Myself *What were you anxious about?*	Starving, anxious	1 lb pasta, 6 croissants, 1 loaf banana bread, quart ice cream, 10 brownies	Yes (V)	Depressed but relieved
Fri 13	9:30	Breakfast	Alone	Irritable	Poached egg, coffee *Excellent protein source but need fat and carbohydrate to feel satisfied.*	No	Good
	1:00	Lunch	Mother	Angry – having fight with mother	Greek salad w/feta cheese, low fat dress ng, 1/2 pita, Diet Coke *Good!*	No *What were you angry about? How can you resolve the feeling?*	Angry
	5:00	Dinner→Binge	Home alone	Still angry at mother	1 lb pasta, 17 meatballs, l pkg dinner rolls, arge bag potato chips, brownies	Yes (V); 3 laxatives	Upset but relieved
Sat 14	8:40	Breakfast	Myself	Resolved to do better	1 cup cereal, 1/2 banana, 1 1/2 cups milk	No	Good
	10:00	Snack	Friend	Good	cup tea, 1 cup yogurt	No	Very good
	12:30	Lunch	Friend Gail	Glad to see Gail	1 scoop tuna salad, lettuce, pita bread, 1 orange	No	
	4:00	Snack	Alone	Hungry	small bag pretzels *Excellent balanced meals! Good job!*		Wanted to purge but didn't – sister there
	6:30	Dinner	Sister-restaurant	In control, happy	1 piece fish, 1 cup rice, 1/2 cup squash *Excellent combination of balanced meals/ good company.*	No	

You seem to be in more control when you are eating with friends that make you feel good. You are making great progress in eating more balanced meals. Notice that the only times you binged and purged were when you deprived yourself during the day on Thursday and when you were angry on Saturday. Good work!

Session 1

Psychoeducational Phase

Objectives for this session: The first session introduces the group leaders and members to one another. It establishes the group contract, presents a historical overview of perceptions and presentations of women's body shape, and introduces the set-point theory as a medical reason for weight-loss diet failure. The group leader(s) issues food logs to members with instructions for their use. The Handout "The Diet Conspiracy" is distributed for discussion in next week's group.

The first session begins with the introduction of the leader(s) of the group and a brief description of the group. Members introduce themselves after the group contract is presented. The group will consist of twelve weekly one and one-half-hour sessions. The purposes of the group include:

1. to become educated about the nature of bulimia nervosa, its etiologies, and its medical, social, and psychological consequences
2. to interrupt bulimic behaviors through meal planning, goal setting, and cognitive-behavioral learned responses and strategies

41

3. to replace bulimic behaviors with healthier and more adaptive responses.

4. to begin to address the relational and interpersonal problems in the members' lives that have resulted in low self esteem, depressed mood, and bulimic symptoms.

The group contract includes the following:

1. each member is expected to attend every session, and when physically unable to attend, the member is expected to inform the leaders of her inability to attend the session prior to that meeting

2. members are expected to arrive on time

3. members are not to leave the meeting place during the group meeting

4. members are expected to respect the confidentiality of each member of the group—anything that is said in the group should stay in the group

5. members are encouraged to talk in the group but will not be "put on the spot"; they are encouraged to participate, because the greater the effort they put into the group, the more they will derive from it

6. outside contact with other members is encouraged to help members develop a support system outside of the therapeutic setting

7. members are expected to be prompt in paying the fee for the group at each session or to provide total payment prior to beginning the series.

After these group expectations are outlined, the members will be asked to introduce themselves by going around the room. They will be offered a chance to say a little bit about what brought them to the group and what they hope to get out of it. They will not be forced to contribute at this first meeting (or at any of them); volunteering this information will be at their own discretion. Some time should be left after these introductions for questions about the group expectations and any other questions pertaining to the group format.

Group leaders then present the historical antecedents of bulimia nervosa and the sociocultural context that prescribes this obsession with thinness. Its content should include the following information (from Anderson and Zinsser 1999; Eisler 1987; Bynum 1987), although each leader may want to adapt or add to it to meet the immediate needs of the members:

What causes contemporary women to have such a preoccupation with shape and weight? Clearly, the trend over the past twenty years has been toward increasingly slim bodies. A look at the historical antecedents of bulimia nervosa may shed some light upon women's current obsession with thinness. In the Paleolithic era, a woman's role was defined as bearer of children and preparer of food. Her body shape and size had significant bearing on her fertility and ability to have children. She, like modern anorectic women, would cease menstruating if her weight dropped to starvation levels. As long as a woman's identity was bound to her role as mother, men and women both desired a woman's body to reflect a mother earth–like image of fertility, health, strength, and survival abilities. Therefore, a full figure was the ideal. (This approval of and desire for robust figures is still evident in certain developing countries today—men are considered good providers and their status is enhanced if their wives have full figures.)

As cultures evolved throughout human history, new concepts of ideal female traits developed. Ancient women were considered

43

attractive and desirable to men if they were young and slender. Women in ancient Crete used drugs that permitted them to be slim while eating as much as they wanted. In Egypt the emphasis on slimness, beauty, and seductiveness in women was reflected in the fashions of upper-status women, which were revealing, close fitting, and impractical.

In the Middle Ages, a number of religious women were revered for their abilities to endure long periods of fasting or deprivation. Part of the ascetic tradition, such "discipline" (as it was termed), provided holy visions and insights. Life stories of medieval female saints often include anecdotes about the saints living on nothing but the Eucharist, or about angels feeding the saint in a vision, with total abstinence from food.

The lean look of the late twentieth century has been in vogue for only about sixty of the past six hundred years. In 1477 Sandro Botticcelli depicted women with large breasts and large bellies that carried the promise of childbearing. By 1700 tastes had changed, and the new ideal was the hourglass figure with small waist, large bust, and large hips. Fashionable women wore enormous bustles after being forced into rigid corsets to achieve this look.

Between 1910 and 1920 fat became unfavorable in Anglo-American culture; the idealized woman was lean and angular. The vogue for thinness, which began around World War One, was initially a sign of emancipation. Women obtained the right to vote in 1920, and many new colleges were providing educational opportunities for women. The popular, slender form of the flapper came to symbolize athleticism, nonreproductive sexuality, and a kind of androgynous independence. A slim woman was considered stylish; she questioned traditional sex roles, read widely, smoked cigarettes, and otherwise

44

established her independence. In the early 1930s, however, came the first outbreak of eating disorders. In the 1940s and 1950s a fuller figure was considered fashionable, but in the 1960s the pendulum swung back to extreme slimness similar to that of the 1920s. From that time until the present, the incidences of anorexia nervosa and bulimia nervosa have been increasing. Notable accelerations have occurred in the past thirty years, following the boom in popularity of extremely thin fashion models like Twiggy (1960s), Bo Derek (1970s), Cindy Crawford (1980s), and Kate Moss (1990s).

Historically, older women have rejected trends toward slimness among the young. During the flapper era, for example, the majority of older women held onto their conservative dress and larger figures and did not participate in wearing tight, short dresses or smoking cigarettes. By the 1960s, however, old age and especially older women had become seriously devalued in media and culture, beginning a trend of older women seeking extreme thinness. The use of cosmetic surgery has increased to preserve a look of slim youthfulness (recall the media fixation about the "novelty" of Katharine Hepburn's choice *not* to have plastic surgery). Cosmetic surgery has become an accepted part of our culture, and by the late 1990's liposuction was the most commonly performed cosmetic procedure in the United States. The worship of youth in the counterculture, in the media, and in most forms of popular culture began to create an insidious form of anxiety in older women, who then began to starve themselves in an attempt to dress and look like their teenage daughters.

It is interesting to note the coincidence of the beginnings of the feminist movement, the emphasis in the media on thinness for women, and the rapid increase in the number of women with

45

eating disorders. The mean age of the bulimic patient population indicates it is the first generation of young women raised at the beginning of the feminist movement. During these years the sociocultural milieu for young women has been in transition and seems to have contributed to gender-role confusion among this age group. Contemporary women are forced to face multiple, ambiguous, and contradictory role expectations.

In a seeming contradiction, a cultural preoccupation with thinness emerged simultaneously with the feminist movement. While the feminist movement certainly did not cause eating disorders, it raised questions about stereotypical gender roles, about definitions of achievement and success for both genders, and about female identity in the context of male-female relationships. In the midst of an increasing focus on achievement and confusion about how to express drive and ambition, the pursuit of thinness may have emerged as one way in which young women could compete among themselves and demonstrate self-control. Paradoxically, the biological and psychological side effects of bulimia and the pursuit of thinness will eventually lead to a state that actually exacerbates the original difficulties of mood instability and low self-image.

Today's media is replete with diet articles. Fashion designers flood women's magazines with unrealistic role models. Compared to the figures these magazines flash before their readers, nearly every woman can perceive herself as overweight. The bodies of fashion models are touted as "normal" (which they very definitively are not), causing increased insecurity about women's opinions of their own bodies (group leaders may want to show advertisements taken from popular magazines to illustrate this trend).

A longitudinal content analysis of fashion advertising in women's magazines in the United States and Europe shows that un-

46

til 1920 full-figured womanhood was glorified. Models were matronly and would be considered fat by today's standards. In the late 1920's, as clothing became more revealing, models became younger and slimmer. While there are many supposed "ideal" female body types in contemporary American culture, all entail extreme thinness. One current ideal is the prepubescent girl with a wrinkle free, taut, immature, thin body. Another is the slender athlete, also taut and thin. Another is the waif model, personified by Kate Moss, who has no muscle tone, is very thin, and is presented to be intensely sexually appealing to men. Imitation of these supposed ideals has led some women to reduce body fat to the point where they are compromising the production of hormones responsible for normal menstrual functioning. The often unperceived irony of these culturally fostered ideals is that these current images of sexual attractiveness in women are actually associated with loss of sexual appetite and reproductive functioning.

After hearing this historical overview, the group is given time to ask questions and to discuss their reactions to it.

Group leaders then introduce the concept of set-point theory (developed by Bennett and Gurin 1982) to explain why repeated dieting is usually unsuccessful in producing long-term change in body weight or shape. According to the set-point theory, there is a control system built into every person dictating how much fat he or she should carry—a kind of thermostat for body fat. And like a thermostat set to maintain a certain temperature, the body's control system has its own set point for fat. Some individuals have a high setting, others have a low one. According to this theory, body fat percentage and body weight are matters of internal controls that are set differently in different people.

47

Going on a weight-loss diet is thus an attempt to overpower the set point. The thin person who attempts to overeat and gain weight is fighting a similar battle. The set point is a seemingly tireless opponent to the dieter. The dieter's only allies are willpower and her chosen incentives, which make chronic physical discomfort worthwhile. But willpower is subject to fatigue, and incentives often lose their value after a time.

The ideal approach to weight control would be a safe method that lowers or raises the set point rather than simply resisting it. So far no one knows for sure how to change the set point, but some theories exist. Of these, regular exercise is the most promising: a sustained increase in physical activity seems to lower the setting (Wilmore et al. 1999). Most people fatten with age, and this may be because they exercise less and their metabolism ultimately decreases (Knox 1999).

According to the set-point theory, the set point itself keeps weight fairly constant, presumably because it has more accurate information about the body's fat stores than the conscious mind can obtain. At least one chemical substance is released by fat cells—leptin. The blood level of this material, which is proportional to the amount of fat being stored, is monitored by the brain's hypothalamus. If the level of leptin falls too low, a complex control system within the brain's hypothalamus somehow begins to compensate. This set-point mechanism may slow the metabolic rate through hormonal and neural signals so that energy is used more sparingly.

At the same time, this system pressures the conscious mind to change behavior, producing feelings of hunger or satiety. Studies show that a person's weight at the set point is optimal for efficient activity and a stable, optimistic mood. When the set point is driven too low, depression and lethargy may set in as a way of slowing the person down and reducing the number of calories expended.

The set point, it would appear, is very good at supervising fat storage, but it cannot tell the difference between a reducing diet and starvation. The dieter who begins a diet with a high set point experiences constant hunger, presumably as part of her body's attempt to restore the status quo. Rare individuals manage to diet and stay relatively thin, despite permanent hunger. Even dedicated dieters, however, often find (to their dismay) that they can not lose as much weight as they would like. After an initial, relatively quick loss of ten or even twenty pounds, dieters often become stuck at a plateau and then lose weight at a much slower rate, although they remain as hungry as ever.

Dieting research, and perhaps personal experience, as well, demonstrates that the body has more than one way to defend its fat stores. Long-term caloric deprivation, in a way that is not clear, acts as a signal for the body to turn down its metabolic rate. Calories are burned more slowly, so that even a meager diet almost suffices to maintain weight. The landmark study *The Biology of Human Starvation*, conducted to gauge and prepare for famine in Europe after World War Two, provides data startlingly similar to physiological descriptions of eating disordered individuals (the obsession with food, for example) (Keys et al. 1950). The metabolic rate, in short, can evidently adjust up or down to correct for deviations from the set point.

The body reacts to stringent dieting as though famine has set in. Within a day or two after semistarvation begins, the metabolic machinery shifts to a cautious regimen designed to conserve the calories it already has on board. The willing spirit is opposed by flesh that is not at all weak; it is perfectly determined to hoard the remaining supply of energy pending nutritional relief. Because of this innate biological response, dieting becomes progressively less effective, and (as generations

49

of dieters have observed) a plateau is reached at which further weight loss seems all but impossible.

After the set point theory is discussed, group leaders should provide opportunity for members to ask questions or voice reactions. Leaders then assign "The Diet Conspiracy" as reading for the next session, emphasizing that members may want to note some reactions to the essay to share at the next meeting.

The next topic is food logs. Leaders should feel free to make copies of the blank food log on page 37 to distrubute to the group. These are explained and distributed to each member of the group. The food log becomes each patient's way of keeping track of the times she eats, what food is consumed, whether she is eating meals or snacks, what her mood and feelings are at the time the food is being consumed, whether or not she purges, and what her mood and feelings are after she purges. These food logs are designed to help each patient become aware of the cues and signals that may precipitate bingeing. Patients also can use the logs as a learning tool to avoid setting themselves up for binges (depriving themselves of food for long periods of time, thus creating voracious hunger, which then results in a binge).

Members are asked to keep careful track in their logs of everything they consume. They are asked to begin the food records the day after the group begins. They will bring the completed record to the group each week and hand them in to the leaders. They will receive written comments and suggestions from the leaders, who will hand the food log back to each member the following week. Food records are not discussed with the group by the leaders. If members want to set goals based on information in the log, they do so at their own discretion.

The group is told that keeping food records is often initially a difficult task to accomplish, but without becoming aware of the actual be-

50

haviors, it is very difficult to modify them. The food log columns identifying the food consumed as a breakfast, lunch, dinner, or snack will help members understand how they define their meals. It may not be obvious to group leaders that a member considers three crackers to be breakfast, so members need to identify each meal as such (B for breakfast, L for lunch, D for dinner, and S for snack). In the appropriate columns, members are asked to describe their moods before and after meals, initially to help them correlate dysphoric moods with binge eating, and to correlate feelings of relief or calm with purging. In this way members will learn that their eating disorders serve to regulate emotions and achieve emotional equilibrium. They are given time to ask questions about these logs; once these questions are answered, the time for the next meeting is confirmed and the group session ends.

51

The Diet Conspiracy

Mary Dockray-Miller

Conspiracy theorists love to pick apart the JFK assassination, the crack epidemic in American cities, or the role of the bureau of Alcohol, Tobacco, and Firearms in the Oklahoma City bombing. Maybe next they should turn their suspicions to the American dieting industry. There isn't actually a conspiracy to keep American women focused on a self-defeating ritual of starvation in pursuit of an unattainable ideal of extreme thinness, but there may as well be. American women spend inordinate amounts of money and time trying to lose weight that, physiologically, they probably can't and shouldn't lose.

Ideal body shape has of course changed over the course of history—put a picture of Marilyn Monroe next to one of Calista Flockhart and Marilyn looks decidedly plump—but the idea that we can work to change our basic body shape one way or another has persisted. Science shows, however, that our ideal body weight (which has little to do with a Hollywood-derived cultural ideal) is somehow "wired in" to our genetics and physiologies, and there is little we can do to change that.

Our culture tends to despise heavy people for their perceived lack of control over their eating habits. The cultural myth depicts overweight people as compulsive eaters who never exercise and who somehow have brought their "fatness" upon themselves. In reality, studies reveal that fat people tend to eat about the same amount as thin people; fat people simply have a higher internal "set-point" than thin people.

"Set-point" is a term popularized by William Bennett and Joel Gurin in their book *The Dieter's Dilemma* (Basic Books 1982). Their analysis, which has since been augmented by other studies, shows that the body monitors the amount of fat reserves it has, increasing or decreasing metabolism (the burning of fat and calories) as needed to maintain that amount of fat. For example: A 5'4" woman weighs 145 pounds. She loses 20 pounds on an eight-week weight-loss diet, greatly reducing her fat and overall food intake. She weighs 125 pounds but is often irritable and tired. Over a period of six months, she replaces the lost 20 pounds. Her body has slowed her metabolism to stabilize itself at her set-point, despite all her efforts.

Bennett and Gurin cite a number of studies which indicate that as the body monitors fat stores, it produces signals of hunger or satiety to keep those stores constant. Research with a variety of populations—conscientious objectors during World War II, prison inmates who volunteered as subjects, military recruits, and volunteers on a liquid diet—all show that the subjects had trouble both losing and gaining weight. In all four populations, subjects reported emotional and mental distress when they forced themselves to gain or lose large amounts (30–50 pounds) of weight. After the studies ended, most subjects' set-points reregulated the body, and the subjects returned to their prestudy weights.

The "trick" to real weight loss, then, is to reset the thermostat, to reconfigure the set-point. While no one is quite sure how to change the set-point, most doctors agree that increased exercise over an extended period of time will effect some sort of permanent increase in metabolic levels. For example, while people have thought that it is inevitable to gain weight with age, physiologists now posit that as people age, they exercise less, and their metabolic rate decreases. The amount of exercise and the length of time needed to effect such a change obviously vary from individual to individual, but it would be wise to listen to health counselors who talk of a "lifestyle change." A life style change means that we cannot view exercise as a temporary measure that is a component of a temporary weight-loss diet; we must see it as an integral part of our lives.

Popular culture has resisted acceptance of set-point theory, possibly because in some way it seems un-American. Our country was built by exploration, hard work, sacrifice, and determination. To be told that there is something we *cannot* change, no matter how "hard" we work, is antithetical to the American mythos of self-creation and self-improvement.

But the set-point is not a well-known, everyday concept for another, more insidious reason. If women accepted their body weights and shapes as normal and physiologically inevitable, then women's magazines would lose much of their editorial and advertising content. Women would not read "Lose Five Pounds the Week Before Christmas," and they would not buy appetite suppressant pills. They would not read "Toning for a Smooth View from Behind" before going out to buy cellulite reduction cream. They would have time, money, and energy spent now on dieting to devote to their careers, their educations, their families, and their friends and themselves. They could write, draw, paint, hike, swim, play.

Maybe it is a conspiracy, after all.

Session 2

Psychoeducational Phase

Objectives for this session: The main focus of this session is instruction in the medical complications of eating disorders. Group leaders need to ensure that members understand the long-term physiological consequences of their disorder. During the session, leaders broach the subject of forming new eating habits, provide a forum for reaction to beginning the work of keeping a food log, and invite discussion of the essay "The Diet Conspiracy." This session is highly didactic, like the previous one, but provides opportunity for some personal reflection and discussion as the members begin to feel comfortable with one another and with the group leaders. The handout "Physical Manifestations of Bulimia Nervosa" is distributed at the end of this session.

The session begins with a discussion of "The Diet Conspiracy." After soliciting initial reactions from group members, the leaders can encourage discussion, if necessary, by using some of these questions:

What are some examples in our culture of the cult of thinness?

What role might fashion magazines play in your lives?

What was your emotional reaction to reading about set-point theory?

55

Have you observed any relationship between your activity level
and mood?

Do you ever feel like you are a victim of popular fashion trends?

The majority of the session is devoted to instruction in the medical
complications of eating disorders. Group leaders present the following information to members, who may take notes and ask questions along the way.
This information is adapted from Becker, Grinspoon, Klibanski, and
Herzog (1991) and Harris (1983). Leaders describe each complication thor-
oughly, answering questions as needed. Leaders should note that while the
mortality rates from bulimia are lower than those from anorexia, members
should consider quite seriously the possibility that bulimia could eventually
kill them (Crow et al. 1999)

The medical consequences of a BN session is divided into categories
based on specific bahaviors, ranging from the complications of intentional
starvation to complications of binge eating, complications of self-induced
vomiting, and complications of cathartic and diuretic drug abuse. Group
leaders take turns discussing each of these categories and distibute the handout "Physical Manifestations of Bulimia Nervosa." A group discussion based
on members' questions follows the presentation by the leaders. Members
should be told that if they have the symptoms discussed, they should seek
the appropriate dental and/or medical care.

I. Complications of intentional starvation

A. Disruption of normal hormone secretion, which can affect
reproductive function and cause

    1. Amenorrhea

    2. Infertility (caused by amenorrhea)

    3. Breast atrophy

    4. Atrophic vaginitis

56

5. Decreased thyroid function (with concomitant lack of energy, weakness, intolerance to cold, and slow heart rate)

6. Predisposition to depression

7. Inability to maintain normal body temperature and loss of shivering response

B. Cardiac disturbances

   1. Decreased heart muscle mass and heart failure

   2. Decreased potassium (can lead to life threatening cardiac arrhythmias)

C. Abnormal kidney function and fluid retention

D. Anemia, decreased white blood cells, decreased platelets

E. Change in bowel habits with constipation, which leads to laxative abuse, dehydration, and electrolyte imbalance. Straining at stool can lead to internal and external hemorrhoids with related pain and bleeding

II. Complications of binge eating

A. Binge eating that follows a period of intentional starvation predisposes patients to greater risk of medical complications than binge eating that follows more normal eating habits.

B. Acute stomach dilatation is rare but fatal. Severe abdominal pain, nausea, and vomiting occur with possible gastric rupture. Gastric rupture has an 80 percent fatality rate

C. Postbinge pancreatitis causes acute abdominal pain that is worsened by lying down, accompanied by fever, fast heart rate, and distention. This condition has a 10 percent fatality rate.

D. Refeeding edema (swelling of hands and feet once normal fluid and food intake resume is caused by the initial lack of protein in the bloodstream)

57

III. Complications of self-induced vomiting

A. Lacerations in oral cavity by inserting objects into the mouth to promote vomiting

B. Bone and soft-tissue bruising of the neck from pressure on the neck

C. Dental abnormalities, including erosion of tooth enamel (leading to tooth decay), tissue and tooth sensitivities, gum disease, and loss of teeth (necessitating caps or crowns)

D. Esophagitis from the action of highly acidic gastric contents on the esophagus. Esophageal strictures may form due to chronic inflammation.

E. Tears of the esophagus (Mallory-Weiss tears) with severe vomiting of blood

F. Esophageal rupture, which leads to circulatory collapse and may cause death

G. Pneumonia caused by aspiration of food into the lungs during vomiting (usually occurs in intoxicated states when the muscles are more relaxed)

H. Severe loss of potassium chloride (found in the stomach) results in weakness, constipation, heart palpitations, fatigue, loss of body water, marked dehydration, and possible shock.

I. Parotid gland enlargement, an unexplained response, is a benign, painless swelling of the parotids. Associated with pancreatic dysfunction, it is usually irreversible.

IV. Complications of cathartic drug abuse (emetics and laxatives)

A. Ipecac, the most commonly abused emetic, can cause severe heart disturbances with arrhythmias and a fatal form of cardiac myopathy.

B. Chronic laxative abuse has a number of results:

    1. Serious depletion of potassium, leading to muscle weakness, cramps, headaches, heart palpitations, abdominal pain, and possible

58

cardiac abnormality (which can cause heart failure and death).

2. Kidney complications, which cause the kidney to hold on to water, causing chronic swelling and bloating.

3. "Cathartic colon," a term for a conversion of the colon into an inert tube incapable of conducting normal peristalsis or of propelling the stool without the aid of large doses of laxatives. This is due to degeneration of the nerves that stimulate the colon to evacuate. At some point not even the laxatives can cause a bowel movement because the nerves they stimulate in the colon are completely damaged.

4. Calcium malabsorption, resulting in osteomalacia and possibly osteoporosis

5. Water weight loss rather than actual weight loss: some patients believe that excessive use of laxatives will purge them of large volumes of food they have consumed. However, by the time the food has gone through the stomach and small intestine and reached the colon, all the calories have been absorbed, so laxatives do not eliminate unwanted calories. Some seeming weight loss may occur because laxatives seriously disrupt water and electrolyte balances, resulting in water loss and dehy-dration.

6. Laxatives are *habit forming!*

V. Complications of diuretic abuse

A. The most common complication is loss of potassium, which (as noted above) leads to weakness, nausea, palpitations, polyuria, excessive thirst, constipation, and abdominal pain.

B. Edema (body swelling) may ensue as a result of the kidney trying to combat dehydration.

C. Dehydration leads to constipation, which may lead to laxative abuse.

59

D. Hypercalcemia, increased uric acid, and loss of sodium are
    electrolyte complications of diuretic abuse.

Leaders hand out "Physical Manifestations of Bulimia Nervosa," a take-home reminder of the medical facts. After this presentation, leaders provide time for discussion that should include the following.

The formation of new eating habits. Leaders introduce the concept that *deprivation leads to bingeing.* Leaders emphasize the long-term goal of adoption of healthy eating habits, with no bingeing or purging.

Hunger response. Members are told that they have to reeducate their bodies to eat in response to hunger. They must gradually learn to tolerate the feelings of fullness and possible temporary weight gain associated with normal eating. The group is encouraged to pay attention to internal signals of hunger and fullness.

Scale discouragement. Leaders discuss the self-defeating nature of the frequent use of scales. Members need to avoid looking to a scale to provide a number that will make them feel that they were successes or failures in their eating habits of the day before. They are encouraged to weigh themselves very infrequently or not at all when they are trying to learn new eating habits. Leaders must emphasize that temporary weight gain is often associated with learning new eating habits; if members continue to look only at numbers they may become discouraged. Leaders should acknowledge the difficulty of not using the scale, even while asking members to try not to use it. This strategy should help to prevent them from feeling like failures if they are unable to stay off the scale for a significant period of time.

Food logs. The group members are then asked to comment on their reactions to the first week of keeping food logs. Leaders will collect the week's log and discuss the review procedure, which is as follows:

    Leaders review each log for patterns of bingeing and purging and

60

also for patterns of improvement.

Leaders try to teach members about connections between emotions and eating by examining the food log for emotional precipitance (to binges or purges).

Leaders should stress that food log analysis is kept confidential; the logs are designed as a tool with which members will start to set goals (a process which starts in week four).

Leaders should be sure to write comments on each log to stimulate each member's thinking about connections between emotions and cating, while at the same time avoiding comments that could be construed as demeaning or insulting to the patient (this can be a fine distinction). Please see the sample food log sheet with comments on page 38.

Leaders will return logs sheets with comments in a discreet and private manner the following week and each week thereafter. We have placed reminders about the food log sheets in each session description; leaders should follow this procedure each week.

Physical Manifestations of Bulimia Nervosa

Face and oral cavity

Enlargement of the parotid glands located on the lateral aspects of
each cheek (irreversible)

Enlargement of the submandibular gland, located under the jaw

Rampant dental decay

Rampant periodontal disease and bleeding gums, with loss of
underlying bone and loss of teeth

Erosion of dental enamel

Cracked skin in corners of the mouth

Skin

Dry skin

Dry hair and hair loss

Hand abrasions

Gastrointestinal

Inflammation of the esophagus

Tears of the esophagus

Vomiting blood

Becker, A. E., S. K. Grinspoon, A. Klibansky, and D. B. Herzog. Current concepts: Eating disorders. *New England Journal of Medicine* 340, no. 14 (April 8, 1999). Reprinted by permission.

Adapted for nonmedical readers.

Stomach bloating due to delayed emptying

Constipation and/or nausea

Excessive gas

Decreased motility of the intestines

Dilatation and rupture of the stomach

Prolapse of the rectum

Heart and blood vessels

Dizziness when rising from sitting or lying position

Abnormalities on electrocardiogram

Cardiomyopathy (enlargement and weakness of heart muscle)
  due to Ipecac poisoning

Cardiac Arrhythmias due to low potassium levels

Endocrine and metabolic

Low potassium levels

Low blood sugar

Irregular menstrual cycles or loss of menses

Osteoporosis

Chronically cold

Low energy

Salt cravings

Obesity

Reproductive System

Infertility

Insufficient weight gain during pregnancy and low birth–weight
  infant

Session 3

Psychoeducational Phase

Objectives for this session: The third session presents a model of balanced nutrition to group members through lecture and discussion about healthy eating habits; that model is then put into practice, to some extent, when the food log sheets from the previous week are returned to individual members. This session illustrates that each group member may struggle with different aspects of the illness, but basic tenets of healthy eating must be learned and gradually incorporated into a person's behavior in order to regulate her eating patterns. The essay "Two Raisinets and a Corn-flake" is assigned at the end of the meeting.

Nutrition and healthy eating. The first half of session three can be led by the group leaders, but it can be especially effective if a guest nutritionist comes for this part of the meeting. The nutrition lecture presents basic information about the spectrum of eating disorders and nutritional requirements for good general health, as well as dispelling myths about dieting and purging as forms of weight control.

Bulimia nervosa is a wide-spectrum disorder, covering a broad range of behaviors with significant possible differences in binge eating-to-purging ratios (the number of times per day or week that individuals

65

engage in these behaviors, from twice per week up to twenty times per day), as well as the methods used for purging (self-induced vomiting, laxatives, emetics, exercise, or starvation).

A balanced diet consists of eating proteins, carbohydrates, and fats from the four basic food groups daily. These well-known food groups are bread, grains, and cereals; fruits and vegetables; meat, fish, poultry, or vegetable proteins; and dairy products. Current nutritional wisdom recommends a pyramid shape to represent these divisions, as a healthy adult eater will eat larger amounts of carbohydrates (the bottom of the pyramid) than she will of fruits, vegetables, or dairy (the middle of the pyramid), and relatively small amounts of fats, oils, and sweets (the tip of the pyramid). Most patients with eating disorders tend to avoid the protein group altogether and try to eat as few carbohydrates as possible. These foods, however, are largely responsible for feelings of fullness and satiety, as well as for the bulk of a healthy diet. Bulimic women tend to lack iron, calcium, and zinc during periods of non-binge eating and overcompensate for these deficiencies during binge eating with food high in sucrose and saturated fat (Gendall et al. 1997).

The Recommended Dietary Allowance (RDA) of protein for adults is approximately 44 to 46 grams per day for females and 56 grams per day for males (i.e., 0.9gms/kg body weight). Protein, crucial for building and repairing tissue and maintaining immune system function, is made of building blocks called *amino acids*, nine of which must be consumed in the diet since they are not produced in the body. Animal products provide high quality, complete protein containing all of the essential amino acids. Protein from plant sources is incomplete (it lacks one or more of the essential amino acids). Grains and legumes contain complementary proteins, which means that they are better sources when they are eaten together (some examples are beans and rice, tortillas with

66

refried beans, or tofu with rice). Good sources of high-quality protein include fish, poultry, eggs, meat, and many dairy products.

Fat is important as a source of fat-soluble vitamins and essential fatty acids. It is required for the body to absorb all fat-soluble vitamins. Fat also provides meal satiety by slowing the emptying of food from the stomach and can actually prevent binge eating by promoting a sense of satisfaction after a meal. The most nutritious sources of fat are those of plant origin, including oils, avocados, seeds, and nuts.

Carbohydrates are the body's primary source of energy. In order for the body to meet the demands of brain and essential nervous system functions, as well as of red-blood cell function, carbohydrates are necessary. Even more energy is needed to fuel the rest of the body. Wide swings in carbohydrate consumption may affect brain function and trigger binge eating. Good sources of carbohydrates include bread and starches, fruit, and many dairy products.

In addition, a balanced diet that includes a variety of foods from all the food groups is the best source of vitamins and minerals. Most vitamins and minerals help the body to utilize energy that is contained in carbohydrates, proteins, and fats. A physician or nutrition counselor may recommend vitamin and/or mineral supplements for group members whose diets are not correctly balanced. This will probably be a daily vitamin/mineral complex that provides up to 100 percent of the United States Recommended Dietary Allowance (USRDA). It is not necessary, or safe, to take higher doses, which can become toxic. The three most important of these minerals are iron, calcium, and potassium.

Lack of iron, the substance in blood that carries oxygen to the cells, can cause anemia, which results in tiredness, weakness, and irritability. Menstruating women are already at risk for iron deficiency, a problem compounded by an eating-disordered patient who avoids iron-rich foods.

67

The RDA for iron is 18 milligrams per day for adult females and 10 milligrams per day for adult males. Good sources of iron include red meat, liver, dried beans and peas, and enriched cereals. Eating a vitamin C–rich food with an iron-rich food promotes iron absorption.

The calcium deprivation frequently seen in eating-disordered patients contributes to the weakness and fragility of bone strength. Calcium is essential for muscles to contract, blood to clot, and for brain and nerves to function. When dietary intake is inadequate, calcium is drawn from the skeleton into the bloodstream to serve these needs. Low bone density is among the most common problems in women with eating disorders. The best sources for calcium are dairy foods, since they provide calcium as well as nutrients such as vitamin D, lactose, and phosphorus, which aid the body in using calcium effectively.

Potassium, along with sodium, regulates the amount of water in cells. It is also important in muscle function and in regulating the acidity (pH) of body fluids. If purging is done by vomiting or laxative or diuretic abuse, the group member can develop life-threatening potassium deficiency (potassium is required for contraction of the heart muscle). Acceptable range for bodily potassium is very narrow, so a high level (induced by pharmaceutical supplements) is equally as dangerous as a low one. Group members should only take potassium supplements if advised to do so by a physician who will monitor potassium levels with blood tests. Safe sources of potassium include bananas, spinach, celery, citrus fruits, and many other vegetables.

When high volumes of salads, fruits, rice cakes, or other nonfilling or non-nutritious foods are consumed, individuals invariably develop cravings for a "quick fix" to quell the hunger pangs that follow. These cravings are a set-up for binge eating. If a person has starved all day or skipped breakfast and had lettuce and an apple for lunch, for example, by mid-afternoon the need to fill up quickly will drive the person to consume large quantities of high carbohydrate and fat-containing foods, such as cookies, potato chips, or ice cream, to fill the void. Thus, what starts as a resolve not to eat or only to "eat light" results in an out-of-control tumble toward the very foods the person is trying to avoid.

Many individuals become so far removed from normal, healthy eating that after months or years of disordered eating, they do not know where to begin making changes. It is very helpful for the nutritionist or group leaders to bring sample portion sizes of some commonly eaten foods and a plate to demonstrate what a "normal" portion of chicken looks like, or a "normal" serving of pasta. Plastic models are available from registered nutritionists and can be a powerful learning tool for members who have no concept of what a normal meal looks like. Members should be encouraged to plan normal meals that meet the goals of the food pyramid rather than face each new day with a fresh resolve not to eat, only to be defeated by the overwhelming urge to binge after depriving themselves of food most of the day.

Members should be made aware that as they begin to increase their food intake and reduce purging (thus beginning the recovery process), they will probably gain a few pounds as the body replenishes lost fluid, muscle mass, and fat. They may feel they are gaining weight too fast, even if they are following recommended nutritional guidelines; the nutritionist or group leaders should assure group members that this initial weight gain will slow down (and probably cease) after the body has replaced its energy stores. Referencing back to the set-point theory and the "Diet Conspiracy" essay can reinforce and personalize this concept for group members.

The most effective way to start a successful day of healthy eating is to begin the day with a nourishing breakfast. Contrary to the disordered

69

mentality that prescribes *not* eating in order to be "good" or attractive, eating a well-balanced breakfast actually provides a sense of control because the day has started without deprivation.

The most important concept presented in this part of the lecture is that *deprivation leads to bingeing*. There is no way to escape this fact. The way to gain control over a day's eating is to begin the day by filling up on nourishing food. The primary step for members wanting to avoid an afternoon binge is to start the day with a breakfast that includes something from each basic group. Most members find that this change is not nearly as hard to make as they fear. At this point in the lecture, the leaders or the nutritionist may want to provide handouts with sample menus for healthy, balanced meals.

The nutritionist or group leaders then address myths, often repeated as truisms, about bingeing and purging as weight control. These are even more insidious than the myth of skipping breakfast because they involve more manipulation of normal physiological functioning.

Myth 1: Bulimic behavior ensures weight loss. Despite the enormous mental energy, time, and anguish spent on these behaviors, the fact remains that most bulimic women are not underweight, and many find themselves hovering around or above normal weight. Purging by vomiting or laxative use is simply not an effective means of weight loss. Although an individual may temporarily feel emotional relief after a purge and regain a sense of control, the loss of calories, water, and electrolytes invariably leads to a signal in the hypothalamus to replenish the lost nutrients. By attempting to stave off eating as long as possible, a frantic craving to fill up rears its head and sets off a binge once again.

Myth 2: Laxatives help the body eliminate all the calories consumed. Purging with laxatives results in no loss of calories. Laxatives work by stimulating smooth muscle fibers in the large intestine. By the time a food

70

bolus reaches the large intestine all the nutrients, proteins, fats, and carbohydrates have already been absorbed by the small intestine and delivered to the bloodstream. Only indigestible cellulose and fiber, along with vast amounts of water and electrolytes, are eliminated through laxative use. Although individuals feel lighter after laxative use, and perhaps "lose" a pound or two according to the scale, the feeling is a result of loss of water and vital electrolytes, not fat or calories. The feeling of control that comes with laxative use, along with the myth that one can eat anything and not pay the caloric consequences, can create a habit that is very difficult to break. Physiologically, the colon also can become dependent on laxatives in order to function, and ultimately it will no longer respond to normal stimuli. Thus laxative use is a highly dangerous and addictive behavior with severe consequences.

Myth 3: Laxatives are essential. Patients often think that laxative use is necessary because regular bowel function is disrupted in most eating disordered individuals. While regular bowel function is disrupted with eating disorders, the cause is often dehydration and inadequate bulk or fiber in the diet. Laxative use temporarily solves the problem of having irregular bowel movements, but it does nothing to provide a long-term, healthy solution. Adding fiber in the form of fiber supplements, such as Metamucil, or other bulking agents followed by adequate fluid intake permits the bowel to act on fiber and to function normally rather than artificially stimulating the smooth muscle through laxative use.

Myth 4: Binge eating can be undone by immediate and complete purging. By the time a binge-eating episode is completed, food has already had time to travel through the stomach, beyond the pyloric sphincter, and into the small intestine. Even vigorous attempts to bring the food up will be in vain. Many individuals with bulimia also report that although they intended to induce vomiting, they may become so tired or

71

feel so hopeless after a large binge that they no longer have the necessary energy or motivation to go through the entire process. This results in the consumption of vast numbers of calories, once again defeating the goal to lose weight.

Myth 5: *Exercise is a safe way to purge*. Purging by means of vigorous exercise is definitively not a safe and reliable method to burn unwanted calories. While healthy exercise in moderation is recommended for nearly everyone, frantic efforts to pursue thinness by spending large portions of the day exercising is neither healthy nor safe. Essential electrolytes are lost through sweating, and dehydration occurs. Furthermore, the body will fight against attempts to lose precious calories needed for normal heart and brain functions. The body defies methods that put such essential functions at risk by slowing down metabolism to hold onto energy stores.

Myth 6: *Patients can stop disordered eating behavior at will*. Studies show that bulimic patients often have an eating disorder for five to eight years before seeking treatment because they believe they can stop bingeing and purging at any time. Patients are often distressed when they realize how entrenched these behaviors become and how difficult it is to give up these habits. The truth of the matter is that disordered eating is an unhealthy solution to underlying emotional problems. Until the underlying feelings are examined and worked through, the behaviors will serve as their own reinforcements. Unexpressed anger, rage, and sadness at past traumas, losses, or emotional and relational conflicts can fuel bulimic behaviors, much to the dismay of the individual who is trying to make things right from the outside in rather than the inside out.

Finally, the nutritionist or group leaders introduce the concept of the Basal Metabolic Index (BMI), which should be 18.5–25. Members can calculate their indices using the following formula and remind themselves that if they are within the range of 18.5–25, their bodies are

72

probably at an ideal weight (which means normal, not fashion-model thin).

The formula:

$$\frac{\text{weight in pounds x 700}}{\text{height in inches}^2}$$

Discussion of nutrition lecture. For the second half of the session, the nutritionist (if one came) should leave the meeting, providing a sense of privacy for discussion about the lecture. Members should be encouraged to comment or ask questions about the nutrition lecture. The leaders can use questions such as the following to stimulate discussion:

What do you know now that you didn't know before?
What was the most important thing you learned?
Were there any surprises in the information you just received?
What is your emotional response to this information?
What physical or emotional cues might you have before or after a binge or purge?

Return of food log sheets. Leaders return the previous week's food log sheets with written comments on each. These comments should encourage members to start to look for patterns in emotional and physical cues that precipitate binges or purges. Leaders then collect the new set of food log sheets (this process is repeated at each of the following meetings). Members sometimes wish to speak to a leader privately about the food log sheets and comments after the group session is over.

At the close of the meeting, leaders assign the essay "Two Raisinets and a Cornflake" as reading for the next session.

73

Two Raisinets and a Corn Flake

Jeanne Loo

I was proud of one thing. I had both mental and physical control over my weight.

I stepped on the scale in the nutritionist's office, and Sue shook her head in frustration. I weighed sixty-nine and one-half pounds. She told me I had to gain two pounds in the next week, or she would put me in the hospital for an eating disorder refeeding program. I pretended to share her concern by nodding my head in agreement. Part of me thought she was right—that my life was in jeopardy. But deep inside I was already thinking of how to lose more weight. It didn't matter that I could very possibly, very soon, die from malnutrition.

I lied to Sue. I told her I never got hungry. The real truth was that I was hungry all the time—morning, noon, and night. Within the hollow emptiness of my stomach, there lay a hungry beast ready to jump out like a roaring tiger completely out of control. If I tempted it with one cookie, the animal would gobble up all my efforts to suppress my appetites for food and anything else related to a healthy body, including love, human relationships, and nourishment. I compelled myself to eat less than 900 calories a day to remain skeleton-thin. I permitted myself to eat two raisinets and one cornflake for breakfast; four pieces of hard candy, fifty carefully counted plain M & Ms, and one pack of sugar-free gum for lunch; and a bag of microwave 94 percent fat-free popcorn for dinner. I was also very good at distracting the hunger beast with hours of compulsive exercise, shopping, cleaning chores, and errand-running.

I put all my waking time and all my mental and physical energy into starvation rituals, because I simply could not wake this sleeping beast that dwelled inside the cage made of bones from my skeleton.

Sue gave me a stack of meal planning sheets with lists of recommended foods. I didn't want to eat according to her guidelines, since I was convinced my own "diet" was the best game I ever played. Right there, I set a goal to fill in the sheets, win the game, and lie about what I had eaten. I decided to compete with Sue, to lie to her and keep the lie secret, and to win the competition by losing more weight.

After I left her office, I knew I had to get home fast to drink some Diet Coke to keep myself from passing out. As much as I loved the high of self-starvation, at times I thought I was losing my mind. I forgot things easily and couldn't think straight. I closed my eyes and fantasized about the two bags of cookies in my cabinet that I kept as a test for myself. I imagined eating every cookie in both bags, knowing all along I'd never let myself lose control like that.

I stopped thinking about cookies and reminded myself about the day I stopped eating. My father had taken my friend Cathy and me to buy new winter coats. She looked gorgeous and sleek and classy in hers. Then, I tried one on, and my father said, "You're getting fat, Jeanne!" From then on, I have constantly reminded myself to put my hand on my stomach to make sure it was flat, to feel my hip bones jutting out on the sides, thinking about Cathy's stomach under her new coat.

Soon after the coat expedition, I discovered I could will my mind into denying hunger. I concentrated on intellectual things, like reading Dostoyevsky till three in the morning, occasionally allowing myself to fantasize about all the food I could have been eating. When I got to seventy-two pounds, I was rushed to Columbia Presbyterian Hospital with bronchitis because my doctor thought it could kill me. My hospital stay taught me new tricks in the food game, like throwing my food away. But the more food I threw away, the more I was throwing away my desire to live in a game of deception and denial.

When my doctors caught this "trick" and insisted I gain at least fifteen pounds, I became frightened of eating real food and putting on real weight. What would become of my reliable dinnertime ritual of eating only a bag of microwave popcorn arranged on a plate in concentric circles? Would I no longer have the comfort and pleasure of counting and eating exactly 240 Cheerios for a bedtime snack?

Being thin for me was a way to zip up my life into a coat of nothingness, devoid of any feelings or desires, related, I suppose, to the coat that made me look fat to my father. The layers of cloth making up the coat smothered me into an emotionless walking zombie from outer space, no longer human. I believed I did not need food, water, or love to function. The danger of starvation didn't phase me in the least. I was beyond all that. And I still am.

Twenty-five years after that hospital incident, twenty-five years after I taped weights to my sweater-covered arms to win the game against Sue, I still want to be as thin as a bird. I think being this thin and tolerating the resulting physical discomfort and loneliness is a lot better than gaining weight and becoming a huge, fat, ugly animal. Over the course of those twenty-five years, I have lost six jobs because malnutrition did not allow me to think straight. I have made serious computer errors that cost my employers a lot of money, and I feel like I have never gotten along with any of my coworkers. I have never socialized, or laughed, or gone out to lunch, or attended parties. But I have stayed thin, and that is most important.

When my work day ends, I walk up Boylston Street, passing by Rebecca's Bakery, Au Bon Pain, Finagle-a-Bagel, Burger King, DeLuca's

Gourmet Grocer, and the Prudential Food Court with its Pizza Hut, Kentucky Fried Chicken, Bay State Chowder, Chinese Panda Express, and Everything Yogurt. Depending on the time of day, the wind direction, and the open doors, alternating scents of honey-glazed doughnuts, French fries, teriyaki chicken wings, and oatmeal bread fill me, I think, just like eating the actual food would, except I stay thin, because being thin matters more than anything else possibly could.

Some days I have to leave Boylston Street quickly and take the orange line home, preferring to be on a foul-smelling train than among the people who can eat at the food emporia on the street. On those days, so potent and real are the scents, so painful the sight of women shopping—menu-planning women with cake boxes and tins and bags packed up with cheeses, breads, and specialty jams—that I have to leave. I am jealous of the healthy women dining so casually, sipping wine and eating shrimp cocktail with their boyfriends.

If I can stay on the street, I like to peer at people eating with the fascination of a person eyeing a foreigner in another country. I know these "normal" people eat in homes and restaurants and go grocery shopping every week. By watching these people and then pressing on, I reinforce a sense of rigid detachment, looking at food, looking at men and, especially, women eating food, pressing my hip bones and my flat stomach, and then moving away. When I can do it and not flee to the train, I consider this feeling essential to my daily existence and sense of power and self-worth. As I said earlier, I am most proud that I have mental and physical control over my weight.

Session 4

Cognitive Behavioral Phase

Objectives for this session: This session begins the members' active participation in and commitment to change through group therapy. In the first three sessions, members largely listened and learned; now they begin to analyze and modify their behaviors through goal setting strategies.

The group leaders begin the session with a discussion about goals that members have had in their lives, using the essay "Two Raisinets and a Cornflake" as a springboard. Members can share their reactions to the essay (with its descriptions of eating rituals, lies, and deceptions) and acknowledge their own eating-disordered goals. Leaders should encourage members to acknowledge such goals ("I want to be the thinnest person in my class"), as well as other goals that may have prompted each member to make changes in her life—to join the group, for example. Leaders may prompt members to begin to reevaluate their goals about appearance and overall success, and to start to separate concepts of appearance and success.

Goal setting. The session begins with a discussion of goals and goal-setting strategies. Leaders should emphasize that weight-loss goals are usually very discouraging, as most group members probably already know. The body's set point usually interferes with dramatic weight-loss goals,

79

such as "I want to lose twenty-five pounds" or "I want to be a size four." Rather than setting a weight-oriented goal (body weight or clothes size), group members should concentrate on setting behavioral goals, which are useful for controlling bingeing and purging.

Goals set by members should be short-term, positive, reasonable, and specific. For example, a useful goal might be "I will take a walk in my neighborhood tonight after dinner for fifteen minutes"; a negative, too general, or unreasonable goal might be "I have to stop being so lazy" or "I'll run five miles a day, every day, for the next three months."

Each member should try to set one goal a day, either the same goal several days in a row or a different goal for each day. The leader should emphasize that if a member does not meet that goal, she should try an easier one; if she is successful, she should go on to a slightly harder one.

Each member should set goals for herself every day; ideally, these goals would build upon each other. Research suggests that goal setting is an important key to success in control over bingeing and purging (see discussion of cognitive behavioral therapy in the introduction).

Problem solving. Leaders should emphasize that members are working toward being their own therapists, spotting their own eating problems, and solving them. Members should use the following problem-solving strategy:
A. Collect data by keeping food records as food intake occurs
B. Analyze the data to identify problematic patterns (the leaders' comments on the food logs model this analysis):

1. Name general problem area (patient feels she is too fat, or she binges when she is too stressed)
2. List specific behaviors that make up the problem
3. List each problem separately
4. Work on one problem at a time

80

C. Brainstorm: look for creative solutions. Members should come up with as many ways as they can think of to solve the problem; they shouldn't worry about whether those solutions are right or wrong just yet. For example, the problem of eating too much at dinner could evoke several solutions:

Slow down, introducing a two-minute delay between courses

Eat in one area without doing anything else

Use low-calorie foods, or prepare foods in ways that use fewer calories

Eliminate certain foods

Decrease portion size

Use smaller plates

D. Members should choose the plan or strategy that seems most appropriate for them without trying to change too many behaviors at once.

E. Members should evaluate their progress periodically, with or without the help of the group leaders. Three points to emphasize about unmet goals and unsolved problems:

1. If a member's plan isn't working, she should adjust it.

2. Members should not criticize themselves for perceived personality flaws or lack of self-control. A member should simply return to Step A of the problem-solving strategy and start over if she did not choose a useful plan, or if her problem is not sufficiently defined.

3. Members should try to be very specific about what interfered with the achievement of a goal and devise a plan of action to prevent that interference. For example, if her unmet goal was to avoid bingeing and purging for one afternoon, she could analyze her food logs, determine that she does not binge and purge if she is not at home, and then make specific plans to be out of the house for the entire afternoon.

81

Food logs and goal setting. Leaders next return last week's food logs with written comments to provide ideas for goals the members might set. Members need to set their goals for the week ahead, thus making the commitment to try to change behavior patterns.

Each member should set at least one goal that is short-term, positive, reasonable, and specific. Some possible goals may be cutting down on the number of binges in a week, bingeing but not purging, or eating only a small portion of a usual binge food. The group leaders should encourage each member to come up with a goal to work on over the next week, going around the room to ask for each goal, discussing each to make it specific and reasonable.

In addition, the group leaders should discuss the possibility of setting other kinds of goals. Just as they can set goals about food, group members can also set them for other areas of difficulty, such as interpersonal relationships or school/work problems. The leaders can ask if any members would like to set a nonfood goal for the week.

Finally, emphasize that when a member meets her goal, she should reward herself. Suggestions for rewards could include buying flowers, taking a bubble bath, starting a new book, seeing a movie, or treating herself to a massage. Leaders may solicit other kinds of rewards from the group to increase the ways in which members can be kind to themselves.

Session 5

Cognitive Behavioral Phase

Objectives for the session: The fifth session focuses on strategies for coping with emotionally stressful situations. The group compiles a list of suggestions of preventive strategies for both general and specific situations (being alone in the evening, for example, or visiting with relatives over the holidays). The handout "Strategies and Suggestions to Prevent Binge Eating" is distributed. The leader introduces the concept of reframing "failure" as a learning experience.

Leaders should note that while the description of this session seems brief, the session's structure encourages detail in members' responses that takes substantial amounts of time. Leaders should concentrate on drawing out narratives and details as members describe personal situations that often result in binge eating. For example, if a member relates that she did not call her mother every day because she usually binges after she calls her mother, the leader could ask the member to describe her relationship with her mother. This response will probably inspire other narratives from other members as well.

Session five opens up the group for discussion of personal situations and encourages the members to participate actively. The first section is a discussion of the outcomes of last week's goal-setting exercise. Group leaders

83

ask each member to report and reflect on her goal and the consequences of her making or not achieving that goal. Questions asked can include:

> Did you work on your goal this past week?
> Were you able to accomplish all or part of your goal?
> What did you do that helped you accomplish your goal?
> How did you feel afterward?
> Did you reward yourself? How?
> If you didn't meet your goal, what got in your way?
> Should you reevaluate the goal to see whether it was too difficult?
> How can you change your goal so you can meet it this week?

Some group members will not have met or even attempted the goals they had set the week before. They may feel ashamed admitting this to the group. Leaders must be very sensitive to the shame aspects of revealing personal failures and should preface this discussion with comments about making failure a learning experience. Leaders should emphasize that group members will all learn from each members' experience whether the goals were met or not. "Failure" should be viewed as an opportunity to learn.

Leaders should emphasize that members are in the group to learn how to change their own behaviors, and that the group is not intended as another opportunity to be perfectionistic or competitive. Members will often learn more from analysis of an unmet goal than from acknowledgment of met goals. It is extremely important to encourage honesty and openness in this process so that the tendency toward a presentation of a false self (for more discussion of the false self, see session eight) is not repeated in the group meetings. It may be difficult for a member to be completely honest in a public setting, because perfectionism, secretiveness, and denial are often an integral part of the problem.

84

The second part of the session engages the members in discussion and creation of cognitive behavioral strategies to prevent binge eating. The leaders go over the "Strategies and Suggestions to Prevent Binge Eating" handout, asking for more specific suggestions and contributions that relate directly to members' life situations. If it is seasonally appropriate, leaders might ask for suggestions about dealing with holiday eating situations.

The session closes with goal setting and food log review. Members should clearly articulate their goals for next week and be aware of patterns that are presenting themselves in their food logs. Ideally, the goals set will reflect the patterns.

Strategies and Suggestions
to Prevent Binge Eating

1. Eat when you're hungry (preferably three meals and two snacks a day).
2. Select foods you feel comfortable eating.
3. Slow down and taste the food you are eating.
4. Do not deprive yourself of food throughout the day.
5. Avoid weighing yourself.
6. Wear comfortable clothing (put away clothes that don't fit, so they are out of sight).
7. Make plans to spend time with others, especially during high-risk binge times.
8. Plan activities that make you feel good about yourself and which provide a sense of accomplishment or connection to others.
9. Make normal eating and exercise, rather than weight loss, your primary focus (weight control will follow naturally from this).
10. Remove yourself from the binge environment.
11. Remind yourself that other people are not as obsessed about your weight as you are.
12. Allow yourself to hold down whatever food you have already eaten (even if it is a "bad" food or if it is "too much" food).
13. Call a friend.
14. Try to avoid bingeing by learning to give to yourself in other ways, like buying yourself fresh flowers.
15. Make the effort to take pleasure in your appearance, and do

things like buying yourself new clothes. You may decide you like changing your image.

16. Avoid bingeing by getting out of the house at your vulnerable times; make plans with the people in your life for these times.

17. Don't let bingeing be the only way for you to "take time off." Find other things that are pleasurable to you, and allow yourself to do them without feeling you must be productive every minute.

18. When you feel the urge, make an effort to remember how bad bingeing and purging makes you feel, physically and mentally.

19. Find other ways to get in touch with and express your feelings; for example, listen to music which matches your mood.

20. If you find you need more structure in your life, like carefully planned meals and activities, take the time to arrange things this way. If you find yourself rebelling against too much structure, experiment with less on a gradual basis.

21. If you do binge or purge, don't tell yourself that you've really blown it and you might as well go all the way. Regard it as a learning experience, a predictable occurrence when change is beginning, and then get back on track.

22. Don't set up your schedule so that bingeing is the only way to avoid chores and studying. Give yourself a break from less pleasant tasks by taking a walk or doing something refreshing, and then reward yourself with a nonfood treat when you finish a chore or a task.

23. Find other things in life that are important to you and devote time to those activities, instead of filling time with eating. Finding other pursuits may require necessary, time-consuming searching.

24. In order not to binge, you must eat. Allow yourself regular meals, so that you won't feel deprived. If you're not used to keeping any food down, begin re-educating your body very, very gradually.

26. Avoid deprivation by allowing yourself to eat reasonable portions of your favorite foods. When you know you can eat cake, it's easier to feel satisfied with one piece because you know you can have it again. It's much better for your health to include foods you really crave in your diet than to make them seem so forbidden that you binge and then purge after eating them.

Session 6

Cognitive Behavioral Phase

Objectives for this session: The sixth session is composed mainly of discussion and analysis of the function served in members' lives by bingeing and purging. Members thus envision their lives without bingeing and purging, using psychodramatic role playing as a tool to facilitate discussion. Since the group is now at its halfway point, members are more comfortable with each other, the group has coalesced, and extended discussion has gradually become a larger part of each session.

Life without bulimia. The group leaders initiate a discussion of the members' relationships with their cycles of bingeing and purging, encouraging members to envision their lives without those cycles.

Questions the leaders might ask include:

What function has the cycle of bingeing and purging served in your life?

What would your life be like without this cycle?

What feelings do you associate with giving up the cycle?

Can you imagine your life without this cycle?

Members thus think about the purposes bingeing and purging serve in their lives. Each member should in turn describe to the group

89

how she thinks her life would be different without her symptoms. During this process, members begin to realize that these eating behaviors function to reduce anxiety—underlying the symptoms of bulimia are often profound losses or injuries to the self that the member is desperately trying to avoid or deny (bulimic women with less severe losses may have milder symptoms or symptoms apparent for a shorter duration).

Examples follow of patients who used bulimic symptoms to insulate themselves from very difficult situations and losses. These examples serve to illustrate the types of feelings and dynamics that may lie beneath the surface of eating-disordered behaviors and are used for discussion.

Example A. A pre-Olympic skier continued to train aggressively on an injured ankle to the point where her ankle was irreparably broken and her hopes for a professional sports career were dashed. An attractive woman, she plunged into a full-blown obsession with dieting and exercise, which eventually led to bulimic behaviors that she felt were out of her control. When she tried to stop binge eating, she became overwhelmingly sad and depressed. These underlying feelings of sadness and anger were for the loss of the sport to which she had dedicated herself for more than a decade. The eating disorder served to prevent her from grieving for her lost career and to focus on external factors over which she felt she had some control.

Example B. A young teenager was in a train accident with her mother. Although they both survived, the mother suffered permanent brain damage and had to live in a nursing home. The young girl still had a living mother but effectively lost all the maternal functions she needed at this vulnerable age. She became obsessed with her own body and looks, and she began to suffer from anorexia nervosa, which led to bulimia when she could no longer deny her hunger. What began as an attempt to need nothing evolved into eating symptoms that consumed

90

her life. At eighty pounds, she came for help and gradually began dealing with the overwhelming loss of her mother, and her symptoms improved.

Example C. A college student had to leave school when her weight fell by twenty pounds. She had always worked very hard and was very well liked by all her teachers for her dedication and hard work. When she began college at a private university, she was completely overwhelmed, and her confidence was destroyed. She called herself "dumb" and "stupid" and felt like a complete failure. She came home and began therapy, where a referral for psychological testing revealed a specific learning disability. She had turned to bulimia to compensate for her lack of control over her grades and school work, deciding that she could achieve a perfect weight if not a perfect transcript. She had great difficulty accepting that learning did not come as easily to her as it did to her siblings, who were at the top of their classes. Once her treatment focused on acceptance of her learning disability and its consequences, she began to improve, realizing that she had strengths that would ensure success in other areas once she redefined her career path.

Example D. Another patient's severe struggle with anorexia and bulimia grew from a terrible dilemma she faced after her father's death. Her mother had become severely depressed and withdrawn, and she was unable to hold a job. After she remarried, her depression lifted and their living conditions improved dramatically. The patient's stepfather had a son who began sexually abusing the patient almost immediately after the marriage. The patient felt ashamed and trapped, fearing that if she told anyone about the abuse she would break up the marriage that had brought her mother back from grief.

For reasons like these, eating disorders serve the important function of keeping the patient distracted with a preoccupation with food and weight, distancing her from overwhelming feelings that threaten the viability of the

91

self. It is key to ask members to envision their lives without an eating disorder because such a life means that they will have to deal with powerful feelings that are harder to face than bingeing and purging

Behavior chains and binge prevention. Group leaders should next emphasize that members do have control over bulimic behavior; they are not helpless puppets destined to binge and purge. Through the group process, some members will gain significant control over, or elimination of, these behaviors, while others will learn some techniques to mitigate the symptoms. Any progress in identifying real issues is a positive step toward gaining control over bulimic behaviors . The expectation is for reduction rather than elimination of symptoms, as some members will need extensive individual therapy to heal old wounds before they can part with their eating disorders altogether. This section of the session is designed to help members identify triggers that lead to binge eating and to develop strategies to avoid those triggers.

Behavior chains are automatic, often unconscious series of behaviors that lead to habit reinforcement. It is helpful for group members to realize that they can have control over their habit if they recognize its cues. Just as an alcoholic man increases the chance that he will drink if he passes a liquor store on his way home from work, a bulimic woman will increase the chance that she will binge and purge if she follows a course that leads only to food.

The leaders should provide the following example (or one more specifically applicable to the member demographic) of a behavior chain:

A college student finishes classes at 3 P.M. She intends to come home every day and go running because she wants to lose weight on her thighs. Once she comes home, the thought of being seen in her running shorts fills her with shame and self-loathing. She decides to have a snack while

92

she avoids putting on her shorts, and every day the snack becomes a binge. She has successfully avoided the humiliation of being seen in her shorts but also guaranteed she will feel humiliated again the next day.

Leaders then ask the group to suggest strategies to help this exemplar break her behavior chain. For next week, each member should bring in a description of her own behavior chain, preferably with a set of specific strategies for breaking it. To facilitate this homework, leaders should ask members to share strategies that have been working for them to prevent bingeing, referring to the work done in session five the previous week. Such strategies would probably include eating three regular meals, exercising regularly, relaxing, and scheduling activities incompatible with binge eating (like taking walks or going swimming.) The leaders should problem-solve with members having difficulty with prevention strategies. To close this section of the session, the leaders can ask if any of the members has additions to the "Strategies and Suggestions" handout discussed the week before.

Psychodramatic role playing. The leaders ask for two volunteers from the group: one to represent the part of the individual that wants to change, one to represent the persuasive power of the eating disorder. The two interact, using specific information about the members' lives as revealed in past group discussions. The leaders should encourage the role players to use situations and desired changes from their own lives. For example, a young woman with an eating disorder who is new to town is invited to a party by a coworker. She has been feeling very lonely and isolated, and she accepts the invitation. The two volunteers enact her feelings when the evening of the party arrives. While getting dressed, she notices that the pants she had planned on wearing feel tighter than

93

they did the last time she put them on. She starts to feel insecure and begins to think about not going.

The eating-disordered role player with bulimia nervosa (hereafter B. N.) might comment: "I don't want to go to that party because everyone will be looking at my fat thighs. They'll think I'm ugly, and no one will want to talk to me." (This thinking is indicative of bulimic thinking. It focuses on appearance rather than personality and assumes that appearance is the only—not even simply the most important—factor in social success.)

The role player who wants to change (hereafter W. C.) then says: "Stop focusing on my weight. I have lots of interesting things to talk about. I can talk about how I just moved here from the South and about my new job and some things I am looking forward to seeing and experiencing in my new town. I can even make social plans with someone I meet at the party to become more integrated into my new community."

B. N.: I know how anxious I get in front of new people. People always judge everybody by their looks. It's not worth feeling uncomfortable and worrying about what they think. I think I'll just stay home. It's safer. I have that ice cream cake in the freezer I've been saving for a treat. I'll have that tonight instead of going to the party.

W. C.: Remember how good you felt when you went to a graduation party, and you met someone who wanted to see the same movie you had been wanting to see, and you ended up going together? Maybe something like that will happen if you go to this party tonight. You might meet a new friend.

At this point, the other members of the group may want to get involved in the role playing as well, associating similar dilemmas in their own lives with the situation at hand. They can contribute to the role play-ing, taking either role as they see fit.

The session closes with goal setting and food log review. Leaders should note that members should wear loose, comfortable clothing at the next meeting for the relaxation exercise. They may also want to bring tape recorders so that they can recreate next week's relaxation session at home.

Session 7

Cognitive Behavioral/Experiential Phase

Objectives for this session: The seventh session provides an opportunity for members to discuss their own behavior chains and their goals for breaking those chains. The behavior chain exercise is tied to food logs and goal setting. In this session, the group sets goals and hands in food logs at the beginning of the group because the group ends after participating in the relaxation exercise. Next, discussion touches upon the relationship between anxiety and bulimia (bingeing and purging usually serve as anxiety relievers). The group then participates in an experiential therapy technique, using visual imagery to achieve relaxation as an alternative to bingeing and purging. The group actively participates in a relaxation exercise led by the group leader, tensing and releasing muscles, using visual imagery to achieve a relaxed state, envisioning a relaxing place, and controlling breathing. The essay "Celebrating Achievement" is assigned for next week.

Goal setting and food log segments are at the beginning of this session. The remainder of the session focuses on the relaxation exercise, ending on the relaxed note that the exercise produces. As part of the discussion of behavior chains (the members' homework from the previous sessions), members continue to refine and extend their goals as they analyze the food logs with the leaders' help.

97

The leaders begin an exploration of the relationship between bulimia and anxiety. In session six, members were asked to envision their lives without bulimic symptoms. Likely responses included an increase of anxiety as a byproduct of giving up the binge-and-purge cycle. To an outsider, the idea that binge eating and purging could serve to reduce anxiety may seem counterintuitive; eating disordered patients are viewed as anxious *because* they have bulimia. In reality, bulimic women often report that as much as they loathe gorging on food and then purging, the relief and sense of calm they experience afterward is very compelling. This reduction in anxiety powerfully reinforces the symptoms of bingeing and purging. The relaxation exercise that follows offers an alternative method to reduce the high tension and anxiety states that precipitate a binge/purge episode. Leaders should thus make sure that members are fully aware of the logic behind the relaxation exercise before beginning it.

If we understand that the bulimic cycle actually reduces anxiety because the individual is diverting intense emotional states, such as anger, disappointment, rage, sadness, loneliness, and self-doubt, into a behavioral cycle, logic dictates that finding alternative ways to reduce states of high tension could obviate the need for the cycle. Bulimia is essentially a manifestation of feelings of enormous emptiness and longing for connection; filling up with food for comfort attempts to fill up the emotional emptiness. Any such practice that results in a marked decrease in anxiety and tension can be difficult to stop: consider alcohol and drug addictions that help individuals relax and forget their life stresses.

While bingeing momentarily fills up the individual and relieves the immediate tension, it is then followed by heightened anxiety at the massive loss of control she has just experienced in the binge. Purging then serves to regain control and bring about a feeling of calm; the patient feels that the damage has been undone and that she is in control.

98

The sheer exhaustion caused by the effort put into the purge can also leave the individual enervated, desiring rest and sleep.

Group members are then introduced to an alternative method to reduce tension and anxiety that has nothing to do with food but everything to do with tuning in to the body and its signals. Research has shown the efficacy of relaxation techniques, specifically massage (Field et al. 1998) and use of visual imagery (Esplen and Garfinkel, 1998), as part of bulimia therapy. Those who have brought tape recorders should turn them on now so that they can recreate the relaxation session at home. While commercial relaxation tapes are available, many members have reported that hearing the group leader's voice at home helps them to reexperience the calm they felt in the group room and to bring them to the desired lower anxiety level.

Members were encouraged last week to wear loose, comfortable clothing to this session. The exercise works best if there is a large floor space where members can lie down. If the group meeting room is not suitable for lying down, members can remain seated in chairs; leaders should emphasize that the exercise is much more relaxing when the listener is lying down. The following is a narrative upon which the leader can base the exercise; the leader may even want to read the narrative in a calm and level voice.

> The relaxation exercise begins with careful attention to breathing. Close your eyes. Think about inhaling and exhaling, the naturally occurring process of breathing. Think only of two words as you think of your breathing. Think "be" as you inhale deeply. Think "calm" as you exhale fully. Be . . . calm. . . . Be . . . calm. . . . Be . . . calm.
>
> (A three to five–minute interval follows in which the members breathe quietly and the room settles down).
>
> Now we will start to relax the muscles of the body, one segment at a time. We'll start at the bottom and work our way up. Tighten

99

the muscles around your right ankle by flexing your ankle and pointing the toes upward. Move the toes as you flex your ankle, then relax. Now flex your left ankle. Move each toe. Relax. Breathe. . . . Be . . . calm. Next, flex your right calf, tensing it and then releasing. Tighten your left calf. Now release. Tighten your right thigh. Now release. Tighten your left thigh. Now release.

Now we'll turn to the arms. Tighten your right hand to a fist. Be calm. Feel the muscles in your right hand and arm contract. Now release; let go of the fist and the tension in the muscles. Now tighten your left hand into a fist. Now release. Be . . . calm. Tighten the muscles of the right upper arm. Now release. Tighten the muscles of the left upper arm. Now release. As you release each tensed muscle, the muscle and the area surrounding it should feel loose and relaxed. Be . . . calm.

Now we will loosen the shoulder muscles. Bring your right shoulder up towards your right ear, tightening all the muscles in that area. Now release and gently let the shoulder fall to a relaxed position. Bring your left shoulder up towards your left ear. Be calm. Release the shoulder and let it fall.

Now we will release tension in the neck. Tilt your head towards your right shoulder, holding it and tensing the neck muscles. Release and bring the head back to center. Repeat that motion on the left, tilting your head towards the left. Tense. Hold. Release, bringing the head back to center. Now raise your chin to your chest, supporting your head with your hands, stretching the muscles in the back of the neck. Think about tightening those muscles one by one. Now release them and let the neck gently down to the floor.

Next, raise your eyebrows, then relax. Do this two or three times. Then, to relax the jaw, open your mouth as widely as possible. Widen your lips and stick your chin out and down. Slowly shift your jaw. You should now feel very relaxed. You have thought about relaxing the major muscles in your body. You are lying down in a quiet room. Be calm. Now we will relax your mind as well as your body. In this relaxed state, you can use visual imagery and see yourself walking along a six-mile beach with fine white sand. It is a warm day, and a gentle breeze cools your back as you walk. You hear the waves gently fall onto the sand, over and over. The water is warm when it touches your feet. Your hair is being gently blown by the breeze. You feel light and calm and relaxed. As you walk along, you see some palm trees in the distance. You walk toward them and then notice a lovely shaded area beneath the trees.

The sand there is a perfect temperature. You decide to lie down on a soft towel and take a rest. You nestle down into the sand and make the contour of your body fit perfectly into the sand by lowering your body down until your entire back is supported and you feel completely held and supported by the sand. You close your eyes and notice the evenness of your breathing and the slow regular beats of your heart. With each inhale you hear the word "be," and with each exhale you hear the word "calm." You sink lower into the sand; you feel the warm breeze and you hear the gentle waves lap upon the shore. Your mind is at rest. Your body is at rest.

Think only about the air you breathe, causing your chest to rise as you inhale and fall as you exhale. You feel easy and light and weightless. You focus only on what is happening at this moment, not on yesterday and not on tomorrow. Focus on the quiet tranquillity that comes from lying here in this safe and peaceful place. Breathe in. Breathe out. Be . . . calm.

You remain in this peaceful spot for a long time. You drift to a deeply calm and peaceful state. You are not sleeping, but you are also not fully awake. You feel yourself floating and drifting to a

101

state where you have no cares and no worries. Breathe in. Breathe out. Breathe in. Breathe out. Be . . . calm.

Now you are slowly beginning to stir. You have been in a very calm state for quite a long time. You begin to feel that newness of energy that you get after a very deep and good sleep. You are beginning to visualize the ocean again, and you feel like approaching the water again, just to walk along the shore where the waves break gently and the breeze blows gently. The breeze is caressing your feet, then your legs, then your torso, then your arms, then your neck, then your head, then the top of your head, and you feel the breeze rustle your hair.

You feel like stretching out your muscles as expansively as you can; you feel like reaching up to energize the muscles. You begin to feel a desire to stand up and to feel the sand beneath your feet. It conforms to the contours of your heel, then the arch of your foot, then each toe. The sand feels so good and warm. You want to walk. You want to feel the breeze blowing in your hair. You want to continue on this beautiful walk where you feel reawakened, calm, light, and free. You want to take this feeling with you as you begin to feel more alert and awake and aware of your surroundings. You want to take this feeling with you as you open your eyes and remember what you have just felt. You want to take this feeling home with you when you leave this room. You will remember that you were able to go to that calm and peaceful place. You can go there again by remembering what we did together here today. You have done this good thing for yourself, and you can continue to do this good thing for yourself when you need to get centered within yourself and find a healthy way to be calm.

Depending on the amount of remaining time and the state of the group, members can choose to talk about the experience or save their comments for next time. Some groups will want to process the experience verbally right away, while others will want to take the relaxed feeling home with them and talk about it next time.

Celebrating Achievement

Mary Dockray-Miller

Summer, 1999. Sports and women didn't always go together the way they seem to now. Young girls are tired of hearing from older women about the bad old days, but it's true that before Title IX really kicked in, a female athlete was something of an oxymoronic freak.

Now I can flop on the couch with my daughter on a Friday night, and we can watch the weekly WNBA broadcast on Lifetime, "Television for Women," as the tagline goes. We watch female commentators and female referees, (mostly) female coaches, and above all the female players. We root for Houston because I was born there but also because the league-champion Comets are on TV a lot. We cheer as Sheryl Swoopes sinks a jumper from way out. She shares a high five with Tina Thompson after she drives into the paint, whirls through the defense, and lays the ball up with sureness off the glass. We watch deft ball handling, no-look passes, three pointers, jump balls—we watch the Comets tear back on defense, and Cynthia Cooper soars into the air, blocks the shot, and heads back down the floor. The camera zooms in on Cooper, who's pumping her hands in her trademark "raise the roof" psych out, and real sweat drips off her chin onto her uniform jersey.

The dead horse of role models and professional opportunity has been beaten hard since the WNBA's first game three years ago, so I won't belabor the exultation I feel when I watch these games with my daughter, who will never know a time when the only place for women in professional team sports was as scantily-clad cheerleaders. I've become interested, now that the first thrill has worn off, in the way that women's sports are marketed and promoted, and in the advertisements that appear during televised women's sports events. Don't get me wrong—I'm still focused on the game—but I've become intrigued as well by commercials for sports apparel and groceries and a myriad of other products, all of which ostensibly celebrate the achievement of female athletics, while, at the same time, assuring the audience that female athletic competency is a part of feminine beauty.

The messages in these advertisements, which bookend Cooper's heroics or Swoopes' defensive maneuvers, is that women's athleticism is most emphatically a subset of their physical attractiveness to men. The bad news is that while my daughter and other girls like her can revel in a fallaway jumper by a professional female athlete, at the commercial break they are shown that, in popular culture, sports ability is simply another fashion accessory in the endless quest for female perfection defined by men. Even in an arena where competence is easy to define— can you break down the defense and put the ball in the hoop?—our culture still focuses on women's looks rather than their abilties.

The women's soccer team's 1999 World Cup win exemplified this tension in women's sports between appearance and performance. Variously dubbed the "soccer babes" or the "babes of summer," the players were sanctified in the American media because they were pretty. We were routinely assured that they could have been models if they hadn't been soccer players. Mia Hamm landed on People Magazine's "Most Beautiful People" list. And it is true that if the players had been ugly, they would not have garnered the media attention that led to 90,000 people watching them beat China in the championship game.

Appearance does matter in our culture. To deny the influence of appearance would be to imagine some utopian society where only performance mattered. Just look at Rebecca Lobo, the glamorous, white, average center for the New York Liberty. Lobo earns more, in salary and endorsements and speaking fees, than all but a few of the other players in the league, although she is not one of the league's ten or fifteen best players. As women in turn of the century America, we need to work realistically toward lessening the importance of appearance rather than idealistically assuming that its impact can be completely nullified.

As women of all colors, shapes, and sizes, we need to ease this tension between appearance and performance. We must fight against cultural trends that value female appearance over female competence—in any arena—sports, education, or business. Women can value their achievements in sports, like skills and competencies in any other aspect of life, as integral and primary facets of themselves, facets that are not related to beauty. One way to make such a change is through athletics, through the use of our bodies to revel in what they can do. We have to stop accepting pop culture's definition of "exercise" as merely a weight-loss methodology and realize that sports are truly about playing well, not looking good. Sports are about performance and achievement at any level of play. Girls like the ones in the sports drinks commercials and women like the ones on the U.S. soccer team can all exult in a good pass, a perfectly timed header, an exhausting practice, or a clutch win.

So I whoop it up when Michelle Timms spins and dishes at the top of the key, and I wish Lisa Leslie would just dunk the ball in a game, and I wonder how my daughter will ease the tension between sports and appearance. I hope she learns, from the U.S. women's soccer team, the WNBA, and her own athletic endeavors, that her body is a tool she can use to achieve athletic feats. I hope she experiences her own triumphs, her own practices, her own physical defeats. I hope she ignores the commercials where boys find girls desirable because the girls play sports and the magazine covers where athletes are made up like models. I hope she doesn't grow to view her athletic accomplishments, whatever they may be, as an extension of her cuteness or as an accessory to making her thin or as a way of being attractive.

Competition isn't necessary for women to make sports into a way for them to achieve and live in their bodies. Athletics performed for pleasure in physical skill, whether a half-mile swim or a two-mile walk or a pickup softball game or world class basketball game, can show women that their bodies are for them to enjoy, not for others to judge. Through sports, we can assert our rights to our bodies on our terms, not on the terms dictated by an insidious and outdated standard of female beauty.

Session 8

Interpersonal/Relational Phase

Objectives for this session: The eighth session focuses on the role of assertiveness and confidence in therapy for bulimia nervosa. Patients discuss the differences between assertiveness and aggressiveness. Leaders set up role-playing exercises to model assertive behavior in anxiety-inducing situations. Leaders solicit situations and examples from members' lives to provide immediate relevance for this exercise. The essay "Celebrating Achievement" is discussed. Leaders inform members that there will be a group meal in session ten, which will be discussed and planned in session nine. The essay "Nourishing the Self" is assigned for session 9.

Members may want to reflect on the relaxation exercise from last time if there was no opportunity to do so during session seven.

Leaders initiate a discussion about the relationship between confidence and bulimic symptoms, soliciting examples of members' experience in social situations that typically lead to binge-and-purge behaviors. Aggressiveness, assertiveness, and passivity should be discussed in detail, with special attention to the primary role of passivity in our culture's shaping of ideal femininity (a reference back to the history section of session one may be helpful here). Bulimic sufferers grow up with

109

the passive parts of themselves continually reinforced (by parents, friends, and culture), so that they are ultimately afraid to be assertive for fear of being disliked.

Mary Pipher and others have documented the loss of self-confidence and self esteem in girls just before puberty (Pipher 1994; AAUW 1992). Young girls in our culture are bombarded by overt and subliminal messages that they should grow up to be compliant, sensitive, passive, and attractive to men. Advertising plays a large part in such a construction (Kilbourne 1999). While women tend to be comfortable asserting themselves by expressing positive feelings, they have much more trouble setting limits or expressing negative or contradictory feelings. Despite enormous gains by the women's movement in the past twenty years, self-assertion does not yet fit comfortably into the standard feminine ideal. Even in our world of female professional athletes, a female National Security Adisor, and female CEOs, women are still judged most strongly by their looks, their marital status, and their children. Feminists debate the existence and direction of the "backlash" against feminism (Faludi 1991; Wolf 1993), but a glance at any mainstream media directed toward women—be it *Vanity Fair* magazine, Lifetime Television, an Oprah Winfrey movie, or www.ivillage.com—shows that appearance and heterosexual pairing are still supposed to be primary female concerns.

Women are taught that they must be passive and compliant in order to be attractive to men, and that it is of utmost importance that they be attractive to men, so it follows that it is important for women to be passive and compliant. Any form of assertiveness or aggressiveness from a woman becomes implicitly unfeminine. Leaders may encourage members to think about language use and connotation regarding assertiveness. While an assertive man is "masterful" (positive connotation), an assertive woman is "strident" (negative connotation)—or maybe just a bitch (a word which has no male equivalent).

110

One result of this construction of femininity for the bulimic patient is the presentation of a false self—stereotypically feminine, nonassertive, and eager to please. The cultural construction of such femininity coincides with the rules of emotional conformity that are learned in these patients' early years of development. Winnicott (1965) has described the child's accommodation to parental needs at the expense of the child's needs as the development of the "false self." Some girls learn at an early age that they are not loved for who they are but for their ability to satisfy their parents' needs for achievement, success, and physical beauty. They discover in themselves a need to live according to external pressures and expectations at the expense of their own needs.

These women are the ones who take on extra responsibilities at work to please the boss but feel guilty about asking for more money as they fear losing favor by appearing demanding. They feel bad about themselves for being angry that others are taking advantage of them, and they feel guilty for having real feelings (especially negative feelings). They continue to present a smiling, pleasing exterior, forever hoping to be "just right." However, the more the false self intrudes, the more distant the woman becomes from her true self. "This person develops in such a way that [s]he reveals only what is expected of [her], and fuses so completely with what [s]he reveals that . . . one could scarcely have guessed how much more there is to [her] behind this 'masked view of herself' " (Miller 1981). Striegel-Moore's research connects the "social self" to propensity to and entrenchment of bulimic symptoms (Striegel-Moore et al. 1993).

Over time, the amassed subconscious anger at being loved for her compliance and achievements at the expense of herself becomes so great that symptoms erupt in the form of bulimia, literally an act of filling her needs (the binge) followed by a violent rejection of having those needs to begin with (the purge).

111

One way to mitigate the demands of the false self is to make group members aware that assertiveness is acceptable, even desirable, and to have them practice assertive behavior in the safety of the group setting. Teaching patients about the importance of mutually satisfying relationships and role-playing examples of ways to get their needs met are essential parts of the relational phase.

> From *Webster's New Twentieth-Century Dictionary*:
> **Aggressive:** 1. tending to assault or invade; starting fights or quarrels. 2. full of enterprise and initiative; bold and active; pushing.
> **Assertive:** characterized by a positive declaration, averment, or affirmation. Similarly, as part of the definition for *assert*: to insist on one's rights, or on being recognized.
> **Passive:** 1. receiving impressions from external agents; not acting; being the object of action rather than the subject. 2. unresisting, not opposing, receiving or suffering without resistance. 3. mentally or physically inactive; lifeless; unenthusiastic; unresponsive.

Leaders can solicit reactions about how these characteristics relate to contemporary ideals of femininity: Why is it that aggression or assertion are typically thought of as "male" traits, while passivity is typically a "female" trait? What are some examples of female roles (in movies, politics, TV shows, advertising, etc.) that substantiate or challenge the equation of femininity with passivity? How do assertiveness and passivity play out in the lives of members? Can we differentiate between assertiveness and aggression? Do members see relationships in their own lives between bulimic behaviors and passivity?

Next, group leaders introduce the concepts of *self-empathy, validation, mutuality,* and *empowerment* (Fedele and Harrington 1990). These are described as mechanisms by which members begin to recognize their

112

true feelings, and the following group exercises will help members begin to articulate their feelings. Leaders set up a role-playing exercise to give members an opportunity to practice assertive behavior. Ideally, role-playing situations will be drawn from members' lives. What follows is an example of a typical situation that can result in binge-and-purge behaviors after passive behavior in a stressful relationship. Two members act out the roles of a group member and her sister. They can role play face-to-face, or, if they find it easier, they can role play "on the phone" at first and not look directly at each other. By the end of the exercise, however, members should be practicing speaking assertively face to face as part of the bulimic woman's search for what Tantillo terms "empowering relationships" (Tantillo 1998). At first, the "member" in the drama is consciously passive, then the scenario is reenacted with assertive behavior.

Passive, nonmutual interaction:

Member: I waited for you for an hour in front of the library, and you never showed up.

Friend: I got hung up at work. You can't believe the stress. I'll never finish this project.

Member: Oh, you're still working on the same report?

Friend: Yes, and I have to learn a new computer program just to do the graphs.

Member: Is that the same report you were working on last week when you didn't show up for the lunch we planned?

Friend: I thought we had been over that! I'm sorry, okay? But you just don't understand how stressful my job is. Your job isn't like that.

Member: Well, okay. Let's plan on getting together this weekend. Are you busy Saturday morning? Maybe we could go to the gym together.

113

Assertive stance, seeking mutual respect:

Member: I waited for you for an hour in front of library, and you never showed up.

Friend: I got hung up at work. You can't believe the stress. I'll never finish this project.

Member: You should have called me. I felt foolish sitting on that bench all that time. (*Self-empathy*) And last week, when we were supposed to meet for lunch, you didn't come then either.

Friend: You don't understand how crazy my job is right now. I feel like I live there.

Member: You need to tell me if you're going to be late or not come when we've arranged to do something. Here's my cell phone number. Call me when you want to get together, okay? (*Empowered response, directly asking for a more respectful exchange.*)

Friend: You're right. (*Validation*) I shouldn't be so preoccupied with my work that I forget that your time is valuable too. (*Mutuality*)

Such a dialogue will elicit discussion from members about their own life situations. As in sessions five and six, the majority of the session is spent drawing out narratives from the members, relating situations from members' lives to one another, and providing suggestions and solutions to help members deal constructively and assertively with those situations.

The session ends with goal setting, food logs, and curriculum reading. When discussing goals and handing out food logs, leaders should ask members to study their food logs and identify feelings that most commonly precede their binge episodes. Members should come prepared to discuss these connections next week. If the feeling is loneliness, for instance, members should try to think of strategies to deal with loneliness that do not involve the use of food.

114

In the time remaining, leaders can ask for reactions to the essay "Celebrating Achievement" in relation to the focus and exercise of this week's session. Some questions could include:

Are there any advertisements you can think of right away that present a passive, stereotypical femininity?

What are some areas besides sports where looks seem to be valued more than competence? How can we recognize and celebrate achievement without focusing on looks?

Is there a connection in your life between exercise and assertiveness?

What is the author's point about the difference between the terms *sports* and *exercise*? Could you see making *sports* a part of your life? In practical terms, how would you do it (i.e., joining a walking club, going to a recreational pickup softball game)?

At the close of the session, leaders ask members to read "Nourishing the Self" for next time, remind them to look for connections between binges and certain feelings (discussed above), and inform members that there will be a group meal in session ten and that they will plan the meal next week.

Nourishing the Self

Mary Dockray-Miller

One thousand years ago, at the beginning of the second millennium, Anglo-Saxon monks and nuns made dictionaries to help them translate Latin, the language of their church, into Old English, the language of their daily lives. They usually glossed the Latin *nutrire* (to nourish) with the Old English *fedan* (to feed), inscribing in the hand-written columns of their dictionaries their and our culture's equation of nourishment with food.

But there is more to nourishment than nutrition and eating. Nourishment also describes emotional and intellectual nurturance. Nourishment promotes our psychological growth. Nourishment is not simply adherence to the guidelines of the food pyramid; it is comfort, support, spiritual sustenance.

Using food to satisfy all of a person's needs for nourishment is ultimately a futile exercise. "Using food" is a phrase akin to "using drugs" or "using alcohol"—food can alter bodily sensation just as marijuana or vodka can. The difference among the phrases is that drug and alcohol users can cut the substance out of their lives. Food users can't. Our physiology requires food. The main similarity among the phrases is that food, drugs, and alcohol can all be used to cover up emotional and spiritual needs that require but have been denied nourishment. While food can fill a person's body, it cannot nourish in other ways. Realizing the futility of using food to fill emotional needs is the primary step in achieving release from dependence on food.

Once a woman confronts this realization—that an all-consuming need for ice cream or a desperate desire for pizza is really a cry for emotional and spiritual nourishment—she opens herself to the possibility of other, nonphysical nourishment, nourishment that will fill emotional and spiritual needs.

Throughout history, much of a woman's femininity has been tied to her ability to nurture others. Women have been valued as mothers of children, wives of husbands, teachers of students, and nurses of patients. All of these roles necessitate the woman's focusing on the needs of others. Women's traditional roles in the family include cook, seamstress, housekeeper, laundress, gardener—roles dedicated to meeting the daily needs of other family members. Now, in the twenty-first century, women still experience a cultural expectation that they nurture others—at the same time that they face professional expectations of career or education. Women need to step outside of these roles, to reject these expectations and give themselves permission to nurture themselves, to nourish their own physical, emotional, and spiritual needs, to recognize those needs as ultimately more important to them than the needs of others. Rather than using food, women can teach themselves to meet their own needs, needs for time alone or for entertainment or for self-care or for developing friendships and relationships.

Women with eating disorders are undernourished in multiple ways. Desire may seem to be for food, but it is actually desire for other, spiritual and emotional, nourishment. Often, food is simply more immediately available than physical intimacy with a partner or a long, solitary walk or a two-hour yoga class or an expensive facial. Once a woman acknowledges her desires and allows herself to have them, she can begin to nourish herself in all dimensions. She can believe that she is important enough to have needs and worthy enough to attend to those needs. To reach this point, she needs to be clear and honest with herself about her desires.

One thousand years after the monks and nuns in their drafty monasteries copied Latin dictionaries with quill pens, we are still looking for the definition of *nutrire*. We must decide for ourselves exactly how to nourish our disparate and sometimes conflicting desires. In one of the old manuscripts—perhaps written by a woman?—there is a hint that the quest for emotional and spiritual nourishment is really nothing new. The Old English gloss for *nutrire* is *weaxan*—to grow, to flourish, to become powerful.

Session 9

Interpersonal/Relational Phase

Objectives for this session: The ninth session focuses on the ability to recognize and express feelings verbally (rather than with food). There is a discussion of the assigned reading from last week, "Nourishing the Self." Examination of the "mood" column in the food logs leads to connections between binge/purge behaviors and certain emotions. Members realize that they are using their relationship with food to avoid recognition of feelings. Leaders encourage discussion about feelings of neediness, deprivation, rejection, sadness, anxiety, and anger; leaders emphasize the importance of being able to recognize and feel these emotions. The group sets final plans for the group meal (next session).

At the beginning of the session, group leader(s) should remind the members that the group meal is scheduled for next week and that the group will be planning the meal during this session. Next, members should be given the opportunity to make comments about last week's session on assertiveness and mutuality in relationships. If a member's goal for the past week focused on assertiveness, she should be asked to share her experience of the week. The other members can comment and relate her experience to instances in their own lives, which will provide validation for her experience and inspire their own quest for mutuality in their relationships.

Leaders remind members that they were asked to reflect over the past week on their food logs to determine their connections between certain feelings that precipitate binges. Research has shown explicit connections between "negative affect" and "compensatory behavior" in bulimic women (Powell and Thelen 1996). Members are now asked to share with the group what they have learned about themselves and their feelings in relation to bulimic symptoms. Moods most often discussed are those of depression, low self-value, and anxiety. The group leader should launch a discussion about feelings behind these moods. Interpersonal theory, as described by Klerman et al. (1984), identified four major domains that contribute to low mood and depression: (1) unresolved grief, (2) interpersonal disputes, (3) role transitions, and (4) interpersonal deficits. Members often feel ashamed about feelings of deprivation (of love, positive regard, admiration, or recognition); they are ashamed to admit feelings of rejection, sadness, anxiety, and anger. Leaders need to reinforce that these feelings are universal, but the degree of shame about them is much more intense in an eating-disordered population because of the pressure to present the self as having no needs in order to be pleasing to others. Members are encouraged to describe their own interpersonal conflicts so that the group can help with problem solving. Most often, group members can easily identify with each others' conflicts. It enhances self-esteem for members to offer helpful suggestions to one another.

Leaders then begin an exercise that sets up a variety of alternatives to binge/purge behaviors. While some ideas will be repeated from the "strategies" brainstorms of session five, these strategies are not only reiterated but analyzed to reveal the emotions underlying the binge/purge

120

behavior. Each member should try to complete at least one of the sentences below, preferably the one that coincides with the member's mood before a binge (as determined by her food log records). Leaders can ask members to finish the sentence on a piece of paper or verbally; completed sentences can then be discussed within the group.

If I am sad, I could. . .
If I am angry, I could. . .
If I am lonely, I could. . .
If I am anxious, I could. . .
If I feel constrained, I could. . .
If I feel empty, I could. . .

Leaders then ask members to visualize themselves enacting this sequence of emotion and action at the beginning of a binge:

1. Stop for a brief moment and try to identify the feeling that seems most important at that moment.
2. Focus on that feeling and try to select an alternative action to help with that feeling.

Members should be encouraged to add this behavioral sequence to their strategies to prevent binge eating. This sequence is more difficult than the strategies discussed in session five because it entails identification of feelings usually suppressed and unacknowledged.

The sections on goals and food logs will usually fit into the flow of the session here because the group discussion about food logs and behaviors presents immediate opportunity to set goals to change behavior. For example, if the goal is "I'm not going to get mad at my sister," it can be modified to be "Instead of bingeing, I'm going to go for a walk and

121

write in my journal while I have angry feelings toward my sister and think about what I need to say to her." This is a reasonable goal and, if met, a successful strategy for dealing with feelings without the use of bulimic behaviors.

Next, leaders ask for reactions to the curriculum reading "Nourishing the Self." Questions could include:

Before you read this essay, did you automatically equate nourishment with food?
Do you feel there are situations where you "use food" like a drug? (This will hearken back to the previous discussion of emotions.)
What are some needs and desires you have that should be met by something other than food?

Preparing the group meal. Leaders should review the concept of the false self from session eight, and then encourage members to share with each other the pressures of falsity in order to please others. Leaders should reiterate the concept that needs and appetites are normal and necessary parts of life. It is not possible to go through life without need for physical and emotional nurturance. Rather than viewing hunger and appetite as bad needs that must be overcome or denied, they must be recognized as signals human bodies employ to sustain life. The idea that food is a necessary and enjoyable fact of existence helps to introduce the group meal and the rationale for bringing food and its concomitant feelings directly into the group room.

The group meal uses the exposure-and-response prevention techniques reported by Gray and Hoage (1990) with brief group therapy, illustrating the anxiety reduction model described by Rosen and Leitenberg (1982). In this model, patients are exposed to stimuli or situ-

122

ations that typically produce the response of anxiety (for bulimic women, that exposure is to foods that trigger binge eating, followed by the anxiety-reducing response of purging). To reduce the response of anxiety, the group voluntarily enters the anxiety-producing situation within the safety of a controlled setting to demonstrate and learn methods of reducing anxiety (relaxation, visualization) different from their usual responses (bingeing and purging).

With about half of the meeting time remaining, members are asked to plan a well-balanced meal together, including carbohydrates, protein, and fats, with a "forbidden food" as descrt. Members should be steered away from a typical meal they might prepare at home (i.e., a protein-poor menu with a salad, low-fat dressing, diet soda, and a few pretzels); instead, they should be asked to plan a meal that will be satisfying and filling. Leaders emphasize that the members should consider the meal as a way for them to be nourished for a few hours rather than as a test to eat only the smallest possible amount to stave off hunger. Leaders should remind members that such a meal will actually diminish the need to binge later because they won't be starving for food by the time they are back home. The members are told that they are expected to remain in the room during the entire meal and are asked to commit verbally not to purge after the meal.

The group meal helps members share a meal together within a supportive atmosphere with others who know how difficult such a situation is for them. Members typically have a great deal of trouble eating before others because of shame about their appetites and because of their need to conform to others' expectations (even though the members feel they cannot meet those expectations). While the use of food logs helps members to recognize and solidify feelings they have experienced about food over each past week, the group meal provides an opportunity to try out some of the cognitive behavioral techniques that they have learned

123

during the group process: eating a balanced meal, taking appropriate portion sizes, being aware of thoughts and ideas about eating that actually conflict with reality (i.e.,"My stomach feels big after this meal, so eating anything makes me fat"). During session ten, members will be encouraged to note the feeling of fullness directly after the meal and to compare that feeling with their sensations one hour later. Such a comparison is a cognitive process that they should also engage in at home so that they learn that *feeling full* is different from *being fat*.

To plan the meal, leaders ask for suggestions from members about what they would like to eat. The members will need help planning a balanced, healthy meal that meets the goals of the food pyramid as discussed in the nutrition session (session three). If the meal is a breakfast, for example, they will need:

- something from the bread and cereal group, such as bagels or dry cereal
- something from the dairy group, such as yogurt or milk
- a fruit or vegetable, such as a fruit salad or berries or bananas; juice counts too
- a protein source (peanut butter, yogurt, or lox)
- some fat, probably from peanut butter, cream cheese, or butter
- a beverage

Although it is breakfast, it is still important to introduce a forbidden food, such as coffee cake or a pastry. All members will be encouraged to eat a portion of the sweet so that they can talk together about the fears, feelings, and cognitions that arise in the context of eating a small "treat" without feeling that they have "blown it" and they might as well binge because they haven't been "good."

If the meal is dinner, for example, they will need:

- a carbohydrate, such as pasta or rice
- a protein source, such as tofu or a store-roasted chicken
- a vegetable source, such as a mixed vegetable salad with dressing
- pita bread or rolls, with margarine or butter
- fruit salad and cookies or brownies for dessert
- a beverage

The members are asked to bring portions of the meal once agreement is made about the meal content. If there are vegetarians or food allergies that preclude a meal that is agreeable to all, special meals can be designated for the member who cannot eat what the rest of the group chooses. Expensive items should be split up by several members so that the burden of the cost falls evenly on all members. A group member can volunteer to bring flowers if it helps to balance the number and cost of the items.

Group leaders volunteer to bring a paper tablecloth, plastic cutlery, paper cups, paper plates, and paper napkins. It is best if the leaders' contributions are in the neutral territory of paper goods rather than food. In this way no extra meaning is given to food the leaders bring. The tendency to please and present the false self increases if the leaders bring food because the members may feel they need to compliment whatever the leaders bring. This could be at the expense of appreciating what the other members have brought. (Group processing of these types of dynamics is beyond the scope of a time-limited group.)

One of the group leaders is responsible for writing down all of the items to illustrate the commitment each member is making to ensure the group meal will occur. If a copy machine is handy, it is helpful for each member to receive a copy, so that she leaves with her commitment in hand and the reminder that the whole group is participating—she is not alone.

125

Session 10

Interpersonal/Relational and Experiential Phase

Objectives for this session: The tenth session is the group meal, an experiential exercise that includes structured eating and experiencing the self in the actual setting in which eating conflicts occur. The session begins with a discussion of the rationale for the group meal. The group explores each member's feelings before, during, and after the meal. Members are required to remain in the group room until the end of the session. The segments on goals and food logs are either integrated into the conversation during the meal or addressed at the end of the session.

Group meal: preparation. The group meal is usually the most anxiety-laden session of the twelve-week course. Therefore, it is important to acknowledge the courage that each member mustered to come to this group meeting and keep the commitment she made to making changes in her eating habits and behaviors. The group leaders reiterate the contract about the group meal, which states that all members remain in the room throughout the meal and that all members have agreed not to purge the meal when they leave the meeting.

    The group meal begins with members setting the table together and arranging the food on serving dishes as a model for eating at home.

127

If, for example, bagels are served, they should be put on a plate or in a basket rather than passed around in a bag. This helps the members to learn that food should be enjoyed visually; in addition, they see the quantity of food chosen and eaten. Such visual reinforcement encourages group members to take responsibility for eating a specific quantity of food. It is easy, especially for an eating-disordered person, to eat bread or snacks out of a bag without keeping track of how much is being consumed, thus avoiding responsibility for consumption. Laying out a portion at the beginning, deciding how much is appropriate for a snack or a meal, is much more psychologically difficult.

Once the table is set and the food placed on the table, the group leaders ask each member to describe how she is feeling and to disclose her current level of anxiety. Many members reveal that they do not know how much food is appropriate to take; they fear they will be judged as "piggish" no matter how much they take. The fear of being judged is pervasive, and the leaders must introduce this fear into the discussion if the members do not bring it up themselves. Some members fear being watched while they eat and have a distorted notion of how interested others are in the way they eat. These feelings sometimes stem from ridicule of eating habits in their families of origin but more likely come from the unconscious belief that having needs and appetites is shameful and base (for a discussion of family mealtime issues and bulimia patients, see Herzog and Sacks 1993). Because many eating-disordered women have been raised to perform well and bring pride and glory to their families while demanding nothing in return, any act that verifies that they have needs is felt as a shameful failure. It is very important that the group leaders speak about the nourishing quality of food and the fact that everyone needs to eat in order to function. To be able to function at the highest level possible, every person must obtain good nutrition to meet the body's demands for essential vitamins and minerals.

128

Group meal: eating. The group leaders act as role models for nutritious eating. They must take appropriate amounts of each of the food items that have been brought in and eat them slowly and with enjoyment. The leaders model eating as a pleasurable experience, talking and socializing with the members to demonstrate the social function of sharing food together. Mention of current movies, news stories, or popular novels would be appropriate as examples of conversation *over* food that is not *about* food.

At the mid-way point through the meal, leaders should ask members to note their anxiety levels compared to the beginning of the meeting. If a member says she is less anxious because the group is talking rather than focusing on how much each member is eating, the leaders can point out that eating provides a social forum for people to get to know one another better, while giving them something to do that is mutually pleasing and healthful.

One of the most valuable aspects of the group meal is the opportunity members have to share their feelings and cognitions about eating *as they are happening* in the group rather than reporting them from memories of the previous week (Franko 1993). Members often associate more freely or remember more about their feelings as they hear their peers talking about food in the group. The group meal also allows the members to try out some of the cognitive behavioral techniques they have learned about, such as sampling "forbidden foods" or monitoring feelings of fullness (often confused with feelings of fatness).

As dessert is passed around, leaders should ask about feelings regarding a cookie or brownie or slice of cake. Members have the option to eat a whole dessert, try a portion, or to decline, but leaders should encourage all members to talk about why they are making that choice. Some members feel that dessert is superfluous and that they do not want the extra calories. Leaders explain that dessert is a "treat" and thus not

129

part of basic nutrition, but that we are all presented with treats of some kind on a regular basis and learning to enjoy food *in moderation* for the sake of the taste and pleasure that it brings is part of having an enjoyable life. Most work or social settings use food to bring people together to celebrate occasions. Allowing oneself to enjoy a piece of cake at a birthday party or a brownie at a coworker's farewell get-together is part of life. Enjoying a great dessert at a restaurant or a relative's homemade coffee cake is part of being in the social world. A key concept modeled at the group meal is that a forbidden food in a small quantity can be eaten and enjoyed without it becoming a portal to an out-of-control binge episode. Members are encouraged to experience the dessert as a way of learning to enjoy a piece of something rather than letting that piece become the first bite toward destruction.

Group meal: aftermath. At the end of the meal, members report for the third time on their anxiety levels. Most feel a great deal less anxious than when they began. They are asked to describe feelings of fullness that they may be experiencing and to talk about how uncomfortable or acceptable that feeling is. Group leaders must remind members that however full they feel, that feeling will pass within an hour or so; they need to congratulate themselves for nourishing themselves the way they did. Group members are reminded that they have contracted to retain the meal they have eaten and that the completion of the group meal exercise depends on their follow-through after they leave the room by abstaining from purging behavior.

Food logs and goal setting. The contents of this section of the meeting may have been a part of the group meal conversation, as a natural part of conversation. If not, this section follows the usual procedures described in previous sessions. Leaders should also encourage each member to list

130

the group meal in her food log along with thoughts and feelings about the experience. Discussion of these food log entries will begin next week's session.

Members are reminded at the end of the session that there are only two sessions remaining. Next week's meeting will offer a time to talk about reactions to the group's ending.

Session 11

Interpersonal/Relational Phase

Objectives for this session: The eleventh session begins the process of ending the group. Discussion of last week's session leads to a discussion of feelings about the group termination and feelings of loss at separating from women with whom they have revealed their authentic selves. Many group members express the desire to have outside relationships that can be as mutually caring and validating as those they have experienced in the group. Leaders present options for continued treatment after termination, meeting briefly with each individual to discuss her needs. The essay "Breaking Down the Prison Walls" is distributed for discussion in session 12.

Reactions to last week. Leaders ask members to share their reactions to last week's group meal, as well as thoughts and feelings recorded in their food logs after the group experience. The variety of responses serves to illustrate that each member is unique, having experienced the group meal somewhat differently. Some members may report a feeling of victory that they were able to eat the meal, accept the feeling of fullness, and not resort to purging behavior. Others may say they felt "bad" for eating the quantity they ate, still not accepting that they need to eat balanced meals.

133

Since the last outcome a leader would want to see is covert compliance coupled with a secret sense of failure and shame (another variant of the "false self"), she must acknowledge that all the members are not at the same degree of readiness to give up their bulimic symptoms. *Being a member of the group and working on symptom reduction and relationships is the goal, not total abstinence from symptoms.*

Food logs and goal setting. This section will probably flow smoothly from discussion of the group meal, as each member recorded the group meal in her food log.

Group affirmation. The acknowledgement of members' differences provides a natural segue for validation of each members' positive qualities. Members are asked to congratulate themselves for joining the group and taking risks during the group process. Leaders ask the members to go around the circle, each member saying something positive about the member on her right. Then the circle is repeated to the left, so that each member will hear two positive comments about herself. This exercise helps to set a tone of acceptance, warmth, and intimacy that ideally mirrors the tone of the group as a whole—an atmosphere that has come about as a function of being together during the group experience and of engaging in a mutually empowering commitment to changing deeply entrenched behaviors.

Reflections on the group process: Leaders ask the members to share reflections about what they have learned, how they feel they have changed, and what goals lie ahead of them after the group cycle ends. Most specifically, members should summarize how their behaviors may have changed over the course of the past eleven weeks.

Leaders can expect a variety of responses. Some members may report that they have been able to reduce their bulimic behaviors substantially

134

during the course of the group to they extent that they have been binge- and purge-free for several weeks. Others may report that, while they have been able to decrease the frequency of the behaviors, they continue to binge and purge. Still others may report that, in addition to decreasing bulimic behaviors, they have learned a great deal about themselves and would like to continue their work in therapy. The group leaders present various options for continued treatment. These options include a variety of treatment modalities, including individual nutrition sessions with a registered dietician, a psychopharmacology consultation, individual psychotherapy, couples' therapy, family therapy, or open-ended group psychotherapy. The group's overlapping phases of psycho-educational, cognitive behavioral, interpersonal, and relational therapies have provided members with an introduction to a variety of therapeutic techniques; they may choose to focus further on the technique that seemed to be most effective for them.

Although many group members make a request that the group continue as a psychotherapy group with the present group members, it is critical to maintain the original contract for a twelve-week integrative group treatment. Members who joined the group chose this particular format for their own reasons; it is not ethical to change the contract of the group even if many members request a continuation. Other members may have been ready for a twelve-week treatment but not for an extended or open-ended group experience. Group pressure may prevent them from having the courage to say so, and in a wish to comply they may say they want the same thing, only to feel coerced and eventually drop out of the group altogether.

If group leaders wish to lead such an ongoing psychotherapy group, the leaders should begin a new group with a new contract after the end of the twelve-week group. This will provide closure for all participants and allow each member to make her own choice about whether to continue in an open-ended group setting.

135

Group members who want to continue in group psychotherapy should certainly be encouraged to do so; leaders can provide referrals to appropriate psychotherapy groups, when available. During the twelve-week group, many individuals are able to gain enough control over their bulimic symptoms and to learn enough about their underlying psychological conflicts that they will benefit greatly from a less structured and more exploratory therapeutic experience. (The concept of a time-limited group as preparation for an open-ended group is described in Riess and Rutan 1992.)

The challenge ahead. Finally, members are asked to identify challenges specific to them, identifying the "red flags" in their lives of people, places, and feelings that have incited bulimic behaviors in the past. Leaders should remind members that while each member has worked hard to make behavioral and attitudinal changes, the important people in their lives have probably not changed at all. Each member should be asked to identify a situation in her life that she knows leads her to bulimic behavior and then to present strategies that will enable her to manage such a situation. This problem-solving exercise reinforces behavioral strategies for realistic situations that will inevitably present themselves as challenges throughout recovery.

Referral conferences. Fifteen minutes of group time (more if there is only one leader) should be reserved at the end for individual consultations about the types of referrals each member would like to receive. In keeping with the practice of maintaining privacy with respect to each individual's food logs, if possible, leaders should discuss each individual's referral needs privately. Each member's continued journey will reflect her own individual and specific needs. At the close of the meeting, leaders ask members to read "Breaking Down the Prison Walls" for the final session in preparation of the group ending.

136

Breaking Down the Prison Walls

Julie Hirsch

I am twenty-seven years old, ten years in recovery, but I don't like to count. I try not to say that "I am a recovering bulimic," because I have found that labels trap me into believing what I believed when I was starving, throwing up, and comparing my body to that of every woman who walked by me. I used to believe I was a beautiful woman simply trapped in my body. My greatest fear was that I would someday become obese. In college, when I was the poster child for recovery and a peer counselor for students with eating disorders, I would fake loving my body. I would listen to the angst of the women who came to talk about their terrible secret for the first time and catch myself comparing my bodies to theirs. I would proclaim in these sessions that women should not be afraid to take up space, while I was actually thinking that it was easy for thin people to say.

Now I know that my body is temporal, banal, and changing. Rented space. I can adorn it and treat it well, so that it serves me well. But I am not my body, I have discovered. When I speak with a friend, it is not my body through which I see her but through my life and my presence, so that I can laugh, listen, and love. When I find myself sticking my body between myself and the world, picturing how my body looks or imagining that it alone defines me, I cannot be free enough to see anything clearly.

This is the prison I built for myself when I was a teenager: I would awaken each morning, happy from my dreams until the reality of what I had eaten the previous evening sunk in. I would trip down the hallway to the scale, the entire day depending on its answer.

I would awaken and wonder about the previous night. On what did I binge? Did I throw up enough not to have gained weight? Did my stomach bloat? Did my fingers swell? I remember the lingering, poisonous taste of the whole bag of ranch potato chips mixed with the acid of vomit.

On other mornings I would have that lovely, lingering high of emptiness, the growling belly, the shaking of my legs as I moved my way down a darkened, carpeted hall to the light of the scale, where there was no morning or night—just:

24 hours since my last binge
2 hours until my next allotted orange
22.5 more pounds to lose
(unknown to me) 4 hours until my next binge
4 hours and 45 minutes until I eat 20 laxatives.

My hungry highs never lasted; my body hated to be hungry. I would binge, and then laxatives would never work. I would strangle a finger down my throat, scrape at the skin with my nails. I remember thinking: "I can't get my finger down far enough for it to work . . . shit, it's not going to work, I'm going to have to digest all this food, all those calories, I can't breathe, my stomach is going to explode." Then I prayed: "Please, let me get it up this one last time, one more chance, and then I'll be good, I won't lose control ever again."

But my body resists the rape of my fingers down my throat, and I curl up onto the corner tile of the bathroom floor, and I feel I am going to die. My mind frantically reconstructs its order, its prison:

5 minutes since my last binge
24 hours until I will let myself eat again.
25 pounds—no, 28—to lose

Some days I can still taste the after-binge in my mouth, feel the food hangover in my belly and throat and fingers. Ten years and the memory remains stored in my body like a scar. But it is not the food I regret. I regret the shadowy moments of damage, the times I took enough diet pills to kill me, when my heart raced so fast I felt it would burst through my chest. Now some days I feel like my body balloons out, while the next day I worry that I am wasting away, and I catch myself falling back into the bulimia prison, for I know things cannot change so quickly.

My body has changed a lot since college. I run to keep myself strong and balanced. My face has thinned out. My stomach is not youthfully tight. My legs are muscular from yoga and running and from my surprised discovery that when I eat what I want, I do not get fat. I still avoid some foods—I eat a chocolate chip cookie and I can feel something brewing in my body; my mind screams for more and more, my body convinced that it is starving, absolutely starving. Then, I need to breathe myself out of the bulimia prison.

I work at a homeless shelter for women in Boston, and there I truly first began to see outside the bulimia prison. The most horrific things I see are the evidences of the traumas the women have experienced. I hear confessions in my office. I witness the complete break of the psyche. And I watch their bodies endure.

I remember having to shower Jennifer my first year at the shelter. She was an obese woman who had been sleeping outside the Prudential building. Inside, I panicked. The 400 pound homeless woman was the embodiment of my worst nightmare, a complete lack of control over the body.

But as I peeled off the clothes she'd worn for weeks, the folds of skin and the smell of infection and the sag to her breasts were just that, bodily attributes. My job was to help clean a body that was unable to care for itself. And there was a woman with stories to tell and the ability to look at me as she sat on the shower seat, naked, and say, "Thank you for helping me."

Another client, Stephanie, spent her labor either holding her breath or screaming into my arm. The eighteen-year-old mother declared she didn't want the baby to come that day. "Let the process happen," I told her. "You can't escape your body." She couldn't, of course, and when I held one of her legs back toward her shoulder, a tiny head appeared, looking alien and purple and not at all like a human being. With another shriek from Stephanie, the rest of tiny Carla emerged, covered in a bloody mesh of membrane and fluid. She was the weirdest and most beautiful thing I'd ever seen. In another five minutes there was a rush of blood and the afterbirth rolled onto the delivery table in a giant wave, another part of the inescapable body. Clients like Stephanie and Jennifer remind me not to rebuild the prison. They uncover the futility of my manic attempts to gain control of my life by structuring my days around the pursuit of a perfect body.

My body will grow old, get sick, and die. It is made of blood and other gross, smelly things. I regret that I spent so much time trying to control my own death, for I have come to believe that I kept my thoughts so frantically centered on thinness and control because I was afraid of what I would see and experience if I let go of delusions and looked at my life. I attempt, now, to experience my life as it is, imperfect and frighteningly unpredictable. And when I am afraid, I just focus on my breath in my body. I breathe.

When I think about my high-school days, I cannot remember how it felt to dance at my prom with a boy I'd had a crush on for eight years. I cannot recall any intellectual awakenings. I was afraid to sing or act and so cannot recall how that felt either. I can only remember the lists of weights and calories, the countdown of time until I would allow myself to eat. I remember the size of the clothes I wore on each school trip but not the destinations of those trips. I can remember whether or not I binged. I was hidden away from the world by my own hand, and I am sad when I think about it. I feel like I am only now learning about how to forge romantic relationships and friendships, how to create good boundaries, how to know what makes me happy. I am happy here now, trying to remember with each step to breathe. I am not my body, I inhabit it. I am not my feelings, but they come and go within me. Everything is constantly changing. With each new experience I breathe and open myself up to it. As long as I do this, the prison walls are gone.

Session 12

Interpersonal/Relational Phase

Objectives for this session: The twelfth session closes the group cycle with open discussion about members' experience in and relationship to the group, evaluation of the group, and information about contacting leaders for future care and referrals. Discussion of the essay "Breaking Down the Prison Walls" helps to end the group cycle on a note of hopefulness, recovery, and optimism.

The final group session is usually an affect-laden experience for the entire group. Members have worked hard to come each week and commit to trying to change their behaviors. They have also taken the risk of breaking the seal of secrecy that has made them suffer in silence for so long. By sharing their secret, they have broken the barrier of isolation that has separated them from others who might understand and care about them. Among the greatest gifts that the group gives the members is a place of acceptance without judgment and validation that legitimate interpersonal struggles have led to the emergence of bulimic symptoms. Because the creation of this safe place has been so meaningful for the individuals in the group, saying goodbye is difficult and sad, as well as joyful and celebratory.

143

Leaders should lead the group in a brief discussion of "Breaking Down the Prison Walls." The closing essay, by a bulimic woman in recovery, provides a good starting point for looking beyond the group sessions. Some questions the group leaders might use to spark discussion include:

Do you identify with the author's remembrances of her binge-and-purge cycles?

Are her "prison walls" similar to the ones you have been breaking down in the past twelve weeks?

Members give to and receive from the group. One of the most important tasks of the last session is to give each member knowledge about herself that she can take with her from the group. In this exercise, members tell each individual what she has given the group; they also tell her what they would like to give her to help her after the group ends. An example of the first might be, "You have given the group the courage to ask for things that we might fear being refused, since you were the one who approached the office manager for overtime pay when you stayed late at work." An example of the second might be, "I would give you self-value and a sense of self-worth for all your hard work and recognition that you do even more than is expected of you."

As the group shares such observations, it becomes clear to everyone how individual and valuable each member's contribution was. In some groups, there are members who were not able to stop bingeing and purging but were still able to come to each meeting. Other members invariably appreciated that person's determination to learn something about herself, even if she was not able to change her behaviors significantly.

144   *Goal setting.* The members relate to each other the last series of goals and

how close they came to meeting them. They go around the familiar circle, sharing with each other how they did last week and what goal they are setting for themselves in the week to come, even though there will not be a group meeting at which they will report. The group leaders emphasize this situation as a way of making real the fact that the group is ending. This process usually produces feelings of sadness that are important to feel and express.

Reinforcement of group therapy techniques as useful strategies after the group has ended. The leaders remind the group that the techniques they have learned to battle their bulimia were not learned only for the duration of the group cycle. The tools they learned to use in the group are ones they can take with them and use regularly on their own. The usefulness of setting small, concrete, and achievable goals is appropriate to a variety of situations and problems in life. Follow-up interviews with group members have revealed that in time of symptom relapse, group members have used food logs and goal setting as a way of getting back on track. Leaders also empower members to take charge of their lives by reminding them of other techniques—using relaxation exercises to decrease anxiety and stress, taking time to recognize feelings and deal with them in constructive ways, using assertiveness to get their needs met, and reviewing medical and nutritional information.

Lapses. Leaders tell members that bulimia is a complicated set of symptoms that often returns during periods of high stress, loss, or conflict. Having an occasional "slip" or relapse is not cause for self-deprecation or alarm but rather a reminder that things have gone off course, emotionally, and that the individual needs to refocus on dealing with her problems directly. A recurrence may last only one weekend, after which the individual will recognize she has healthier tools to use than her

145

bulimic symptoms. A longer relapse may indicate a need for further therapy if the relapse cannot be brought under control. Group members are reminded that bulimia was part of their lives for a long time before they came for treatment and that unlearning these behaviors may continue to be challenging and at times difficult. They are asked if they are all comfortable with the recommendations and referrals that they received last week and are told how to contact the leaders if they need other referrals in the future.

Closure. The group members are usually very comfortable talking together by this point, and often the goodbye session is led more by what the members have to say to one another than through facilitation by the leaders. Leaders must understand the emotional implications of the members' saying goodbye to the group and not risk filling time with so much information that the members are not able to express what they have meant to one another in the group. If time permits, or if the members are unusually withdrawn, the leader may end the group by asking each member to share the most valuable thing she learned. Most frequently, this material emerges spontaneously from the members and does not have to be extracted by the leader.

The last few minutes of the final session consist of the leaders thanking the members for their participation in the group. A few words about the leaders' feelings are appropriate as well, as each group has its own special dynamics and complexion. The leaders can share what struck them as unique or special about this group. The group ends with the leaders wishing the members well in their future endeavors.

146

Conclusion

The group therapy described in the previous sections of this manual and variations of it have been offered at Massachusetts General Hospital, in Boston, for many years. While hundreds of women with eating disorders have been treated with group therapy, the following data reflect the efficacy of six specific groups of bulimic women who completed a course of integrative therapy. Pilot data were drawn from female patients ranging in age from twenty-one to forty years old. Data showed two important improvements: (1) The average number of binge-purge episodes per week in the month preceding group therapy decreased by at least 60 percent, with many patients reaching full remission by the end of group treatment; (2) The mean Beck Depression Inventory (BDI) score prior to group therapy decreased by eight points, moving patient from the scores representing moderate depression to mild depression. (For complete statistical information, see Riess 2002.)

The improvement seen immediately following group therapy and the ease with which the approach was implemented indicate that this treatment approach can have wide applicability. The reduction in scores on the postgroup BDI suggests that there is something powerful about the group process that helps to alleviate depression. Typically, social

147

support and adjustment in women with active BN are remarkably low. They have fewer people in their social networks able to provide emotional support than women in remission or in control subjects. Women with BN are especially dissatisfied with the quality of emotional support provided by relatives. This dissatisfaction may be exacerbated by the deficits in social skills and assertiveness so often seen in bulimic women, who have difficulty articulating their needs (Rorty, Yager et al. 1999). Because of their paucity of social supports and interpersonal skills, the patients in this population benefit greatly from the validation offered by this group treatment.

The interpersonal and relational therapeutic components of the integrative group model provide a holding environment that encourages discussions of conflict and problem solving. Members have an opportunity to try new assertive responses to interpersonal dilemmas by role playing and by allowing themselves to receive support from one another. Members bring relational and interpersonal challenges to the group that are impediments to their growth in their workplaces, as well as in their personal lives. The decrease in helplessness and increase in empowerment that comes with group support and discovery of new solutions to problems each contribute to higher self-esteem.

Because the integrative group model exposes patients to several therapeutic methods, it is especially useful in helping members identify which specific approach will be most helpful to them in the future, if setbacks occur or if they elect to pursue further treatment at the end of the twelve sessions. With the many treatment options reported in the eating disorders literature, a future goal remains in identifying the most effective treatment for the greatest number of patients that face this vexing disorder.

Future research on the effectiveness of the integrative approach outlined in this manual could include focus on the separate phases as they

Conclusion

relate to different population groups: Which segments of the treatment were most effective for which populations? Do age, occupation, social class, severity of symptoms, or geographic setting influence treatment efficacy? Other important populations for whom clinical trials could be conducted could include men (perhaps cohorts of wrestlers or weight-lifters), patients currently treated with antidepressant medication, groups of women over the age of forty, girls ranging in age from fourteen to eighteen, and groups that have—or have not—received therapy for eating disorders previously. Further research could focus on long-term effects (one year and five years post-therapy) of this approach. The twelve-session therapy efficacy could also be tested against nonintegrative twelve-session therapies.

We close the manual by encouraging leaders to reflect on their own strengths and conceptualizations of the mutative elements of group therapy as they guide patients through this integrative treatment. All effective treatments require warmth, empathy, and nonjudgmental acceptance on the part of the leader. It is our hope that participating in these groups will yield a rich and diverse experience to all of the individuals receiving and leading this form of therapy.

149

Bibliography

The American Association of University Women (AAUW)
Educational Foundation. (1992). *How Schools Shortchange Girls*.
Washington, D.C.: AAUW Educational Foundation.

American Psychiatric Association. (1994). *Diagnostic and Statistical
Manual of Mental Disorders*. Fourth edition. Washington, D.C.:
Author.

Anderson, B. and J. Zinsser. (1999). *A History of Their Own*. Revised
first edition. New York and London: Oxford University Press.

Apple, R. F. (1999). Interpersonal therapy for bulimia nervosa. *Journal
of Clinical Psychology* 55 (6): 715–725.

Barth, D. and V. Wurman. (1986). Group therapy with bulimic
women: A self-psychological approach. *International Journal of
Eating Disorders* 5 (4): 735–45.

Becker, A. E., S. K. Grinspoon, A. Klibanski, and D. B. Herzog.
(1999). Eating disorders. *The New England Journal of Medicine*
340:1092–98.

Becker, A. E., R. A. Burwell, S. Gilman, D. B. Herzog, and P.
Hamburg. (2001). The impact of television on disordered eating in
Fiji. *The British Journal of Psychiatry,* in Press.

Bennett, W. and J. Gurin. (1982). *The Dieter's Dilemma*. New York:
Basic Books.

Beuf, A., R. Dglugash, and E. Eininger. (1976). Anorexia nervosa: A sociocultural approach. Manuscript, University of Pennsylvania.

Blouin, J., K. Schnarre, J. Carter, A. Blouin, L. Tener, C. Zuro, and J. Barlow. (1995). Factors affecting dropout rate from cognitive-behavioral group treatment for bulimia nervosa. *International Journal of Eating Disorders* 17:323–29.

Boskind-Lodahl, M. and W. C. White. (1976). Cinderella's step-sisters: A feminist perspective on anorexia nervosa and bulimia. *Signs: A Journal of Women's Culture* 2:342–55.

Brotman, A. W., A. Alonso, and D. B. Herzog. (1986). Group therapy for bulimia: Clinical experience and practical recommendations. *Group* 9 (l): 15–23.

Browning, W. N. (1985). Long-term dynamic group therapy with bulimic patients: A clinical discussion. In S. W. Emmett, ed., *Theory and Treatment of Anorexia Nervosa and Bulimia: A Biomedical, Sociocultural and Psychological Perspective,* pp. 141–53. New York: Brunner/Mazel.

Bruch, H. (1973). *Eating Disorders: Obesity, Anorexia Nervosa and the Person Within.* New York: Basic Books.

Brumberg, J. J. (1988). *Fasting Girls.* Cambridge, Mass.: Harvard University Press.

Bulik, C. M., P. F. Sullivan, F. A. Carter, V. V. McIntosh, and P. R. Joyce. (1999). Predictors of rapid and sustained response to cognitive-behavioral therapy for bulimia nervosa. *International Journal of Eating Disorders* 26:137–44.

— (1998). Predictors of one-year treatment outcome in bulimia nervosa. *Comparative Psychiatry* 39:206–14.

Bynum, C. W. (1987). *Holy Feast and Holy Fast: The Religious Significance of Food to Medieval Women.* Berkeley: University of California Press.

Connors, M. E., C. L. Johnson, M. K. Stuckey. (1984). Treatment of bulimia with brief psychoeducational group therapy. *American Journal of Psychiatry* 141:1512–16.

Cooper, P. J., S. Coker, and C. Fleming. (1996). An evaluation of the efficacy of supervised cognitive behavioral self-help [for] bulimia nervosa. *Journal of Psychosomatic Research* 40:281–87.

Crago, M., C. M. Shisslak, and L. S. Estes. (1996). Eating disturbances among American minority groups: A review. *International Journal of Eating Disorders* 20:239–48.

Crow, S., B. Praus, and P. Thuras. (1999). Mortality from eating disorders: A five- to ten-year record linkage study. *International Journal of Eating Disorders,* 26 (1): 97–101.

Doerr, P., M. Fichter, K. M. Pirke, and R. Lund. (1980). Relationship between weight gain and hypothalamic pituitary adrenal function in patients with anorexia nervosa. *Journal of Steroid Biochemistry* 13:529–37.

Eckert, E. D. (1985). Characteristics of anorexia nervosa. In J. E. Mitchell, ed., *Anorexia Nervosa and Bulimia: Diagnosis and Treatment,* pp. 3–28. Minneapolis: University of Minnesota Press.

Eisler, R. (1987). *The Chalice and the Blade: Our History, Our Future.* New York: HarperSanFrancisco.

Esplen, M. J. and P. E. Garfinkel. (1998). Guided imagery treatment to promote self-soothing in bulimia nervosa. *Journal of Psychotherapy Practice and Research* 7 (2): 102–18.

Fairburn, C. G. (1981). A cognitive behavioral approach to the management of bulimia. *Psychological Medicine* 11:707–11.

— (1985). Cognitive-behavioral treatment for bulimia. In D. M. Garner and P. E. Garfinkel, eds., *Handbook of Psychotherapy for Anorexia Nervosa and Bulimia,* pp. 160–92. New York: Guilford Press.

— (1993). Interpersonal psychotherapy for bulimia nervosa. In G. R. Klerman and M. M. Weissman, eds., *New Applications of*

Interpersonal Psychotherapy, pp. 353–78. Washington, D.C.: American Psychiatric Press.

— (1997). Interpersonal psychotherapy for bulimia nervosa. In D. M. Garner and P. E. Garfinkle, eds., *Handbook of Treatment for Eating Disorders*. Second edition, pp. 278–94. New York: Guilford Press.

Fairburn, C. G., R. Jones, R. C. Peveler, S. J. Carr, and R. A. Solomon. (1991). Three psychological treatments for bulimia nervosa. *Archives of General Psychiatry* 48:463–69.

Fairburn, C. G., W. S. Agras, and G. T. Wilson. (1992). The research on the treatment of bulimia nervosa: Practical and theoretical implications. In G. H. Anderson and S. H. Kennedy, eds., *The Biology of Feast and Famine: Relevance to Eating Disorders*, pp. 318–40. New York: Academic Press.

Fairburn, C. G., R. Jones, R. C. Peveler, R. A. Hope, and M. O'Connor. (1993). Psychotherapy and Bulimia Nervosa: Longer-term effects of interpersonal psychotherapy, behavior therapy, and cognitive behavior therapy. *Archives of General Psychiatry* 50:419–28.

Fairburn, C. G., M. D. Marcus, and G. T. Wilson. (1993). Cognitive-behavioral therapy for binge eating and bulimia nervosa: A comprehensive treatment manual. In C. G. Fairburn and G. T. Wilson, eds., *Binge Eating: Nature, Assessment, and Treatment*, pp. 361–404. New York: Guilford Press.

Faludi, S. (1991). *Backlash*. New York: Crown.

Fedele, N. and E. A. Harrington. (1990). Women's groups: How connections heal. *Work in Progress* 47. Wellesley, Mass.: Stone Center.

Field, T., S. Schanberg, C. Kuhn, T. Field, K. Fierro, T. Henteleff, C. Mueller, R. Yando, S. Shaw, and I. Burman. (1998). Bulimic adolescents benefit from massage therapy. *Adolescence* 33:555–63.

Franko, D. L. (1993). The use of a group meal in the brief group therapy of bulimia nervosa. *International Journal of Group Psychotherapy* 43:237–42.

Gard, M. C. E. and C. P. Freeman. (1996). The dismantling of a myth: A review of eating disorders and socioeconomic status. *International Journal of Eating Disorders* 20:1–12.

Garfinkel, P. E. and D. M. Garner. (1982). *Anorexia Nervosa: A Multidimentional Perspective.* New York: Brunner/Mazel.

Garner, D. M., W. Rockert, M. P. Olmstead, C. L. Johnson, and D. V. Coscina. (1985). Psychoeducational principles in the treatment of bulimia and anorexia nervosa. In D. M. Garner and P. E. Garfinkel, eds., *Handbook of Psychotherapy for Anorexia Nervosa and Bulimia*, pp. 513–72. New York: Guilford Press.

Gendall, K. A., P. E. Sullivan, P. R. Joyce, F. A. Carter, and C. M. Bulik. (1997). The nutrient intake of women with bulimia nervosa. *International Journal of Eating Disorders* 21 (2):115–27.

Gray, J. J. and C. M. Hoage. (1990). Bulimia nervosa: Group behavior therapy with exposure plus response prevention. *Psychological Reports* 66:667–74.

Grunebaum, H. and L. Solomon. (1982). Toward a theory of peer relationships: II. On the stages of social development and their relationship to group therapy. *International Journal of Group Psychotherapy* 32:283–307.

Halmi, K. A., J. R. Falk, and E. Schwartz. (1981). Binge eating and vomiting: A survey of a college population. *Psychological Medicine* 11:697–700.

Harris, R. T. (1983) Bulimarexia and related serious eating disorders with medical complications. *Annals of Internal Medicine* 99 (6): 800–807.

Hay, P. and C. Fairburn. (1998). The validity of the *DSM-IV* scheme for classifying bulimic eating disorders. *International Journal of Eating Disorders* 23:7–15.

154

Herzog, D. B. (1988). Eating disorders. In A. Nicholi, ed., *Harvard Guide to Modern Psychiatry,* pp. 4344–445. Cambridge, Mass.: Harvard University Press.

— (1982). Bulima: The secretive syndrome. *Psychosomatics* 23:481–87.

Hornyak, L. M and E. K. Baker. (1989). *Experiential Therapies for Eating Disorders.* New York: Guilford Press.

Johnson, C. and M. E. Connors. (1987). *The Etiology and Treatment of Bulimia Nervosa: A Biopsychosocial Perspective.* New York: Basic Books.

Jones, D. L., M. M. Fox, H. M. Babigian, H. E. Hutton. (1980). Epidemiology of anorexia nervosa in Monroe County, New York: 1960–1979. *Psychosomatic Medicine* 42:551–58.

Kaye, W. H., M. H. Ebert, H. E. Gwirtsman, and S. R. Weiss. (1984). Differences in brain serotonergic metabolism between nonbulimic and bulimic patients with anorexia nervosa. *American Journal of Psychiatry* 141:1598–601.

Keys, A., J. Brozek, A. Herschel, O. Mickelsen, and H. Taylor. (1950). *The Biology of Human Starvation.* Minneapolis: University of Minnesota Press.

Kilbourne, J. (1999). *Deadly Persuasion: Why Women and Girls Must Fight the Addictive Power of Advertising.* New York: Free Press.

Kirkley, B. G., J. A. Schneider, S. W. Agras, and J. A. Bachman. (1985). Comparison of two group treatments for bulimia. *Journal of Consulting and Clinical Psychology* 53 (l): 43–48.

Klerman, G. L., M. M. Weissman, B. J. Rounsaville, and E. S. Chevron. (1984). *Interpersonal Psychotherapy of Depression.* New York: Basic Books.

Knox, R. A. (1999, Sept. 27). Deflating a myth. *The Boston Globe,* p. Fo1.

Lacey, J. H. (1983). Bulimia nervosa, binge eating and psychogenic

155

vomiting: A controlled treatment study and long-term outcome. *British Medical Journal* 286:1609–613.

Leszcz, M. (1992). The interpersonal approach to group psycho-therapy. *International Journal of Group Psychotherapy* 42:37–62.

Levenkron, S. (1978). *The Best Little Girl in the World*. New York: Warner Books.

Miller, A. (1981) *The Drama of the Gifted Child*. Second edition. R. Ward, trans. New York: Basic Books.

Miller, D. A., K. McCluskey-Fawcett, and L. M. Irving. (1993). Correlates of bulimia nervosa: Early family mealtime experiences. *Adolesence* 28:621–35.

Miller, J. B. (1988). Connections, disconnections, and violations. *Work in Progress* 22. Wellesley, Mass.: Stone Center.

Minuchin, S., B. L. Rosman, and L. Baker. (1978). *Psychosomatic Families: Anorexia Nervosa in Context*. Cambridge, Mass.: Harvard University Press.

Morton, R. (1985). Phthisiologica: Or a treatise of consumptions. In A. E. Anderson, ed., *Practical Comprehensive Treatment of Anorexia Nervosa and Bulimia*. Baltimore: The Johns Hopkins University Press. (Original work published 1694, in London, by S. Smith and B. Walford.)

Olmsted, M. P., R. Davis, D. M. Garner, W. Rockert, M. J. Irvine, and M. Eagle. (1991). Efficacy of a brief group psychoeducational intervention for bulimia nervosa. *Behavioral Research and Therapy* 29:71–83.

Ordman, A. N. and D. S. Kirshenbaum. (1986). Bulimia: Assessment of eating, psychological adjustment, and familial characteristics. *International Journal of Eating Disorders* 5:865–78.

Peterson, C. B. and J. E. Mitchell. (1999). Psychosocial and

156

pharmacological treatment of eating disorders: A review of research findings. *Journal of Clinical Psychology* 55:685–97.

Pike, K. M. and B. T. Walsh. (1996). Ethnicity and eating disorders. *Psychopharmacology Bulletin* 32:265–74.

Pipher, M. (1994). *Reviving Ophelia.* New York: Ballantine.

Pope, H. G., J. L. Hudson, and D. Yurgelun-Todd. (1984). Anorexia nervosa and bulimia among three hundred women shoppers. *American Journal of Psychiatry* 141:292–94.

Powell, A. L. and M. H. Thelen. (1996). Emotions and cognitions associated with bingeing and weight control behavior in bulimia. *Journal of Psychosomatic Research* 40:317–28.

Pyle, R. L., J. Mitchell, D. Hatsukami, and F. Goff. (1984). The interruption of bulimic behaviors. *Psychiatric Clinics of North America* 7 (20):275–86.

Riess, H. (2002). Integrative time-limited group therapy for bulimia nervosa. *International Journal of Group Psychotherapy* 52 (1).

Riess, H. and J. S. Rutan. (1992). Group therapy for eating disorders: A step-wise approach. *Group* 16:79–83.

Rorty, M., J. Yager, J. G. Buckwalter, E. Rossotto. (1999). Social support, social adjustment, and recovery states in bulimia nervosa. *International Journal of Eating Isdorders* 26 (1): 1–12.

Rosen, J. C. and H. Leitenberg. (1982). Bulimia nervosa: Treatment with exposure and response prevention. *Behavior Therapy* 13:117–24.

Roy-Byrne, P., K. Lee-Benner, and J. Yager. (1984). Group therapy for bulimia: A year's perspective. *International Journal of Eating Disorders* 3:97–116.

Russell, G. M. (1979). Bulimia nervosa: An ominous variant of anorexia nervosa. *Psychological Medicine* 9:429–48.

Rutan, J. S., A. Alonso, and J. E. Groves. (1988). Understanding

157

defenses in group psychotherapy. *International Journal of Group Psychotherapy* 38:459–72.

Safron, J. O. and Z. V. Segal. (1990). *Interpersonal Process in Cognitive Therapy*. New York: Basic Books.

Schmidt, U. and J. Tresure. (1997). *Clinician's Guide to Getting Better Bit(e) by Bit(e)*. East Sussex, UK: Psychology Press.

Schneider, J. A. and S. W. Agras. (1985). A cognitive behavioral group treatment for bulimia. *British Journal of Psychiatry* 146:66–69.

Spangler, D. L. (1999). Cognitive-behavioral therapy for bulimia nervosa: An illustration. *Journal of Clinical Psychology* 55:699–713.

Steiner-Adair, C. (1991). When the body speaks: Girls, eating disorders, and psychotherapy. In C. Gilliagn, A. Rogers, and D. Tolman, eds., *Women, Girls, and Psychotherapy: Reframing Resistance*, pp. 253–66. New York: Harrington Park Press.

Stevens, E. V. and J. D. Salisbury. (1984). Group therapy for bulimia adults. *American Journal of Orthopsychiatry* 54:156–61.

Stice, E. (1999). Clinical implications of psychosocial research on bulimia nervosa and binge-eating disorder. *Journal of Clinical Psychology* 55:675–83.

Strangler, R. S. and A. M. Printz. (1980). *DSM-III*: Psychiatric diagnosis in a university population. *American Journal of Psychiatry* 137:937–40.

Striegel-Moore, R. H., L. R. Silberstein, and J. Rodin. (1993). The social self in bulimia nervosa: Public self-consciousness, social anxiety, and perceived fraudulence. *Journal of Abnormal Psychology* 102:297–303.

Sullivan, P. F., C. M. Bulik, and K. S. Kendler. (1998). The epidemiology and classification of bulimia nervosa. *Psychological Medicine* 28:599–610.

Surrey, J. L. (1991). Eating patterns as a reflection of women's

158

development. In J. V. Jordan, A. G. Kaplan, J. B. Miller, I. P. Stiver, and J. L. Surrey, eds., *Women's Growth in Connection*. New York: The Guilford Press.

— (1987). Relationship and empowerment. *Work in Progress* 30. Wellesley, Mass.: Stone Center.

Tantillo, M. (1998). A relational approach to group therapy for women with bulimia nervosa: Moving from understanding to action. International Journal of Group Psychotherapy 48:477–98.

Thiels, C., U. Schmidt, J. Treasure, and R. Garthe. (1998). Guided self-change for bulimia nervosa incorporating use of a self-care manual. *American Journal of Psychiatry* 155:947–53.

Treasure, J. L., U. Schmidt, N. Troop, J. Tiller, G. Todd, and S. Turnbull. (1996). Sequential treatment for bulimia nervosa incorporating a self-care manual. *British Journal of Psychiatry* 168:94–98.

Treasure, J. L., M. Katzman, U. Schmidt, N. Troop, G. Todd, and P. de Silva. (1999). Engagement and outcome in the treatment of bulimia nervosa: First phase of a sequential design comparing motivation enhancement therapy and cognitive behavioral therapy. *Behavior Research and Therapy* 37:405–18.

Waller, G. (1997). Drop-out and failure to engage in individual outpatient cognitive behavior therapy for bulimic disorders. *International Journal of Eating Disorders* 22:35–41.

Weiss, L. and M Katzman. (1984). Group treatment for bulimic women. *Arizona Medicine* 41:100–104.

White, J. M. (1999). The development and clinical testing of an outpatient program for women with bulimia nervosa. *Archives of Psychiatric Nursing* 13:179–91.

Wilfley, D. E., W. S. Agras, C. F. Telch, E. M. Rossiter, J. A. Schneider, A. G. Cole, L. Sifford, and S. Raeburn. (1993). Group

159

cognitive-behavioral therapy and group interpersonal therapy for the nonpurging bulimic individual: A controlled comparison. *Journal of Consulting and Clinical Psychology* 61:296–305.

Wilfley, D. E. and L. R. Cohen. (1997). Psychological treatment of bulimia nervosa and binge eating disorder. *Psychopharmacology Bulletin* 33:437–54.

Wilmore, J. H., J. P. Despres, P. R. Stanforth, S. Mandel, T. Rice, J. Gagnon, A. S. Leon, D. C. Rao, J. S. Skinner, and C. Bouchard. (1999). Alterations in body weight and composition consequent to twenty weeks of endurance training. *American Journal of Clinical Nutrition* 70:346–52.

Wilson, G. T. (1999). Cognitive behavior therapy for eating disorders: Progress and problems. *Behavior Research and Therapy* 37 (Supplement): S79–95.

Wilson, G. T., K. L. Loeb, B. T. Walsh, E. Labouvie, E. Petkova, X. Liu, and C. Waternaux. (1999). Psychological versus pharmacological treatments of bulimia nervosa: Predictors and processes of change. *Journal of Consulting and Clinical Psychology* 67:451–59.

Winnicott, D. W. (1965). *Ego Distortion in Terms of True and False Self: Maturational Processes and the Facilitating Environment.* New York: International Universities Press.

Wolchik, S. A., L. Weiss, and M. A. Katzman. (1986). An empirically validated short-term psychoeducational group treatment program for bulimia. *International Journal of Eating Disorders* 5 (l): 21–34.

Wolf, N. (1991). *The Beauty Myth.* New York: William Morrow.

— (1993). *Fire with Fire.* New York: Random House.

Yalom. I. D. (1985). *The Theory and Practice of Group Psychotherapy.* Third edition. New York: Basic Books.

160